Hell
ON 4 PAWS

Hell

ON 4 PAWS

A story of love, life and Chesil,
the delinquent dog

Gwen Bailey

hamlyn

An Hachette UK Company
www.hachette.co.uk

First published in Great Britain in 2010 by
Hamlyn, a division of Octopus Publishing Group Ltd
Endeavour House
189 Shaftesbury Avenue
London
WC2H 8JY
www.octopusbooks.co.uk

ISBN 978-0-600-62176-8

A CIP catalogue record for this book is available from the British
Library

Printed and bound in the UK

10 9 8 7 6 5 4 3

Inside cover photos courtesy of the author.

For Chesil and all rescued dogs, as well as those
still in need of a new home.

Acknowledgements

I would like to thank Grant and Holly for allowing me to share their stories with the world. I would especially like to thank Grant for doing all the right things to help us work on Chesil's rehabilitation, from supporting me emotionally to learning new ways of acting with dogs.

I would also like to thank my editor, Trevor Davies, who believed in the book from the outset and cleverly didn't tell me how many words I would need to write until I had written most of them, and also my copy-editor, Dawn Bates, who cajoled me into revealing much more of my story than I would otherwise have done and skilfully moulded my words into good English. Thank you to both of you for your support during the delicate process of helping me get what I wanted to say down on paper.

My thanks also go to those people who read the manuscript, for your great suggestions and encouraging enthusiasm – John Hoerner, Lea Hoerner, Karen Ingram, and Nicky Brunt.

And, of course, this book could not have been written without Chesil, Spider and all the dogs I have known, loved and learnt from, and who have brought such joy and colour to my life. I hope this book will help owners to understand their dogs better and play some part in returning the favour to dogs everywhere.

Contents

Chapter 1

Trouble on a frosty night

I KNEW I loved the man, but could I ever learn to love his dog? This was just one of the negative thoughts running through my head at 3 am as I stood naked in his garden, acutely aware of the deep, rumbling growl of a dog somewhere very close by. I couldn't see her in the gloom, but I knew she was near enough to do some serious damage if I continued to advance.

I hadn't expected to be outside when I had come downstairs or I would have put on some clothes. My dog Spider, a large and lovely Beauceron, needed to go out to the toilet and had woken me by resting his head gently beside me on the bed. So I had left Grant sleeping and had come downstairs, half asleep myself, and opened the back door. Spider trotted out and Chesil, the newly arrived Chesapeake Bay Retriever, seizing her opportunity, had bulldozed her way past me and disappeared into the garden with him. Spider quickly returned and I waited patiently for Chesil to come back in. I called, and I waited, then I called again ... and waited. Eventually, already a little chilled, I ventured out into the pitch black, freezing cold night air to see where she had got to.

Although Chesil was new to us, Grant and I had been together for nine months and I knew he was the person I wanted to spend the rest of my life with. I have always had better relationships with dogs than humans, understanding them in a way that seemed second nature. Humans, on the other hand, with their power to deceive and be intentionally cruel, I was less comfortable with and I struggled with issues of trust and commitment. Grant had been different from the rest, soothing my worries and creating a place of safety where I wanted to stay. When we met, I knew that he had been what I was looking for. He was kind and communicative, with a strength of character that had matched mine, allowing us to form an equal partnership. He had a deep laugh that I could locate him by if I lost him in a building, and an easy smile that had me hooked from the first moment. We had been inseparable since that first meeting and there had been a nine-month window where everything had been tinged with the all-encompassing happiness that comes with new love.

There were issues, of course, as there always had been for me. One was his house, which he had bought soon after I met him. He had moved out of a delightful, old-stone rented cottage, which I loved and felt at home in, into what I labelled the 'retirement home'. It was a large house, built for a retired couple, in its own plot of land in a lovely village, but the style was one I associated with old age and grandparents. Technically, there was nothing wrong with the house, but it didn't seem to fit Grant or our future life together, and I felt uncomfortable and out of place there. Even a good makeover couldn't save it and I resisted settling down there, despite Grant's frequent invitations to move in. So I commuted every day, from my house where I worked, to his house where I lived and slept. I kept few possessions there and so every weekend packed up vast amounts of belongings that I might need, like a homeless person, together with Spider who always went everywhere with me.

Another issue, of a more recent nature, was Chesil. Stinky, aggressive, bad-mannered, annoying Chesil, an unwelcome relic and reminder of Grant's previous life, who had arrived into our relationship like a tornado. She was now somewhere out there in the darkness. I couldn't just leave her as she couldn't be trusted not to escape from the garden – I knew I had to brave the cold and dark to go and get her back in so we could all go back to bed.

Outside the back door, the garden is lit by a warmth-activated light. When it sprang into life as my warm, unclothed body, now rapidly losing heat, went past, I could see that Chesil was not in the main part of the garden, which meant that she had gone round the corner of the house where it is darker. Thinking that it would be a quick job to get her back in, I padded along the back of the house, my bare feet on freezing cold paving, hoping that the high fences would protect my modesty from any neighbours who happened to be awake and looking out of their windows at that time of the night.

I discovered Chesil sitting beside the gate leading to the front garden. She was watching me with eyes that shone in the faint light from the main garden, and I could see from her huge pupils, glowing red in the dark, that she was already in an agitated state. I called her and she didn't move, so I moved forward to take her collar to lead her gently back into the house. She gave a deep, thunderous growl. Reacting too slowly to heed her warning, my fingers closed around her collar, and I felt her teeth bite down on my wrist. She applied a strong, crushing pressure, not fast enough to break the skin but hard enough to cause steadily increasing pain until I was forced to let go. She was good at this – it was clearly a technique she had used before.

I was really annoyed by her reaction. I'm used to dogs that I live with being willing to cooperate and work with me, in the same way that I work to make them feel happy and comfortable. Chesil had scared me with her unreasonable reaction and I resented such an unjust response to my simple request. On top of that, she was very lucky that we had taken her on in the first place and had no right to be making life difficult for me when I was only trying to help. I felt she should, at the very least, be trying to control herself as she was a guest in our house. As a dog, she had no sense of guilt about putting people out. I knew that, of course, but it wasn't easy to be professional at that time in the morning.

I was losing heat fast and the prospect of getting back inside seemed very appealing, not least because I was concerned that the commotion would attract amused viewers to a show I had not intended to put on. I knew Chesil was worried about being shut in the kitchen alone, so worried that she would prefer to curl up in a freezing garden for the night. Although part of me felt it would serve her right, I knew I wouldn't be able to sleep if I left her to spend the rest of the night on the cold concrete. Besides, she may decide to break out of the garden when it got light and go on a rampage through the village, so I felt I had no choice but to get her in by some means.

I began telling her off in a cross, but not-too-loud voice, more of an angry stage-whisper, hoping it was enough to persuade her to see the error of her ways and not wake Grant or the neighbours. It was then that the heat-sensor light went out. Not being able to see me in the total darkness, she started a low, rumbling growl. With jaws that I had seen breaking bone, I didn't want to be too close, so I retreated a little. Frustration and temper then took over – 'How dare you be so naughty,' I shrieked as loudly as I dared, going round behind her with the intention of shooing her forwards towards the door.

If I had been thinking straight at that time in the morning, I would have known better than to leave the house to retrieve an untrained, unpredictable dog without taking a lead. I could have clipped on the lead without her getting agitated and quietly led her back to the kitchen. To fetch a lead now would require another journey across the back of the house on cold concrete in bare feet in full view of the neighbours, and so shooing seemed a more favourable option, albeit an unprofessional one.

Chesil responded to my anger by moving away swiftly, knowing from the tone of my voice that I meant business. As she shot round the corner of the house and passed by the back door, she triggered the light. I got to the corner of the house just in time to be fully bathed in its glow and to see her tail disappearing underneath the garden table in between the chair legs. She could have gone back into the kitchen. That would have been an easier option as the door was still wide open and closer but, no, she decided that squeezing under the table was preferable. Chesil had only been with us for a few months. Before that, because of her difficult and unruly behaviour, she had spent her time in a small kitchen, getting very little exercise, going for every scrap of food she could find. As a result of this lifestyle, she was grossly overweight and only fractionally smaller than the table she was attempting to hide under.

In her previous home, Chesil had been known to terrorize the women of the household. In fact, there were only women in the household so they were both terrorized. I felt she needed to learn that it was possible for a woman to get the upper hand, even a naked one in the middle of the night, and I knew it was important to not allow her to 'win' when she resorted to aggression as she had done in the past. For this reason, and partly because I was naked and freezing cold, I decided that the only way to get her out from under the table was to get the broad-headed mop from the house and push her until she was forced out into the open, from which I could herd her back into the kitchen. This wasn't very professional, but I really wanted to be back in a warm bed now and my tired brain could not think of another way to get her out. So I fetched the mop and attempted to push her big, heavy body out from its hiding place. The prodding brought much angry resistance in the form of growls initially, escalating to high-pitched yelps and squeaks as she realized that she might actually lose the battle and have to come out from under the table. She was furiously attacking the mop and making a terrible racket.

At this point, the window opened above us and Grant's sleepy face appeared. I really wanted to speed this up now as I knew he would come down and try to take charge of the situation. Dogs were my business, not his. I was the one who was supposed to be the dog expert and I wanted to be seen to behave competently with dogs at all times, even at 3 am. I wanted to prove to Grant that I could cope with his unruly mutt, so I became more frantic with the prodding to try to get her out until I heard a snap, which was the sound of the head breaking off the pole of his plastic mop.

A few seconds later, he appeared in the kitchen doorway and shouted at the top of his voice, 'Chesil! Get inside!' Grant has an incredibly loud voice and when he shouts, he can be heard over long distances. Close up, it was like thunder. Chesil stopped growling and squeaking immediately, and obediently trotted inside. Head down, tail lowered, but doing exactly what he had ordered. 'Dammit,' I thought, 'one to him and the "shouting at your dog" technique,' and zero to me with all my knowledge and desire to practise kind methods,' even though I was too tired, cold and agitated to think of them while naked in a frosty garden in the middle of the night.

'I thought there was a fox or something under the table,' Grant said as we headed for the stairs. 'With all that yelping, I thought it had got trapped and you were trying to set it free.' Having heard how aggressive Chesil had been in the past and having been on the receiving end of her aggression a few times already, I have to say I would rather have faced a trapped fox than Chesil under the table. I decided to wait and tell him, in the morning, that I had broken his mop.

Chapter 2
Good credentials

MY DEFINITION of a rescue dog is one that has had to live with more than one owner and, at some point, faced an uncertain future. There have been other rescue dogs in my life before Chesil, many thousands in fact. As well as taking on and rehabilitating problem dogs of my own, I worked for one of the UK's biggest animal welfare charities for 12 years, helping other owners to understand their dog's behavioural problems and put them right, and teaching staff how to rehabilitate rescue dogs. I'd been a consultant for many animal rescues centres around the country, dealing, eventually, with particularly problematic dogs where the choice was to rehome or euthanize. My worldwide courses and lectures helped rescue centres that were less experienced in behaviour knowledge to improve their procedures and place more dogs more successfully.

Despite all my experience, no dog was as difficult for me as Chesil. She wasn't technically difficult, in the sense that I didn't know why she behaved as she did or how to cure her, but she was emotionally difficult, arriving at a time in my life when I wasn't ready to take her on. As well as bad timing, a bigger problem was that she really wasn't a lovable dog. Her unique combination of genetics and past experiences had made her into something very rare – a dog I just didn't like. She was pushy, aggressive, fat, rude and smelly, with a will of iron and absolutely no manners. Added to this, she was extremely aggressive over things she had taken or stolen, and, worst of all, had a nasty habit of rolling in her own urine, and anything else disgusting she could find on a walk – for Chesil, the stinkier it was, the better. When this was combined with her strong natural odour, it made her quite easily the most smelliest dog I have ever come across. Even when bathed, the sweet smell of the shampoo, together with the residual odour from her skin, created a sickly combination that was slightly worse than the original smell alone.

Chesil was as wide as a house, which made her an unstoppable battering ram if she wanted to get past you. Due to her excess eating, she made a very unpleasant smelly mess right in front of you as soon as she went into the garden, no matter how often she was let out, and squatted down to urinate as soon as her paws hit the grass, not thinking to move away to a more remote part of the garden. I tried to keep an open mind, but she simply wasn't a dog you could feel sorry for. When I first met her, I was glad she wasn't my dog. When I found out that there was a chance she would become mine by association, I knew it was going to take all my skill and knowledge to make her into something resembling a dog I could love and live with. She definitely wasn't a project I wanted to take on.

The negative feelings I had towards Chesil were alien to me as I could usually see the good in even the most unruly, aggressive dog and love it despite its behaviour. Dogs with a bad attitude are usually misunderstood, lovely creatures, just waiting for someone to understand and help, and I could always see through their bravado and glimpse the kind of dog they could be with a little work. I wondered if I was being influenced by the fact that Chesil was Grant's ex-wife's dog, with all the connotations that brought, but when I described Chesil's personality to friends, they understood why I didn't like her.

My best friend Helen had met Chesil in person and, although she loves dogs, she also found it difficult to like her. As soon as I had brought Chesil in to where Helen was sitting, she had tried to push her stinky body onto her, pushing with all her strength and trying to force Helen backwards. When this had failed, she tried to rake at her with her claws, gaining attention from Helen in the form of wounded squeaks as she had intended. She tried to jealously push in between Helen and Spider as Helen tried to greet her doggy friend, causing aggravation and upset to all. All in all, it hadn't gone well and Helen was sympathetic when she heard that I was likely to have to live with Chesil permanently. I wondered just how I was going to help rehabilitate this dog when I knew from my many years of experience that you needed an open heart, and love and patience by the bucket load, in order to make progress.

Throughout my life, I've been lucky enough to get on well with all animals. This isn't magic or a special gift, but simply an aptitude for understanding what they might be thinking and being aware of what could alarm or upset them. This ability developed during my childhood years when I spent time with any animal I could find, preferring them to the rather unkind humans I often encountered. I also have a very visual brain, being interested in pictures more than words, and I've noticed that people that are good with animals have a similar capacity, perhaps finding it easier to read the subtle signs and clues animals give to help you gauge their thoughts and feelings. My parents had taught me compassion for animals from an early age, expressing disapproval if I was unkind to one of my many pets and asking me to consider what it must feel like to be on the receiving end of my actions.

When I was very young, I remember the German Shepherd 'guard dog' from next-door squeezing through a hole in the fence and rushing towards my little black mongrel and me as we sat in the garden. I'd heard terrible reports about this dog, how it had bitten its owner and was 'dangerous', and had often heard the owner raging and shouting at the dog while it barked ferociously. Fearing that the huge beast racing towards us might be about to eat my pet, I calmly got up in time to intercept him, blocked him with my body and took his collar. After an initial struggle, during which he realized I wasn't going to let go (I'd have given my life to protect my little dog, and had no fear of being bitten at that age), he gave up and allowed me to lead him gently back to his very startled owner's front door. I remember talking quietly to him as we walked, a little afraid now that the crisis had passed, but finding that this lovely gigantic dog – silky, soft and gentle – responded to my voice with a gently wagging tail. As I gave him back to his angry owner, I felt a wave of regret that I hadn't allowed him his freedom for longer.

I didn't know it then but this natural affinity with animals would lead to a long and rewarding career working with dogs. As a teenager I worked tirelessly and happily in a local breeding and boarding kennels during weekends and holidays. Life at the kennels was an amazing education for me, teaching me the skills so necessary for my future work, like how to approach frightened dogs and gain their trust by keeping still and not making eye contact. I learnt that frightened dogs don't like to have your hands too near them and to only touch them when they 'invite' you to do so by making close contact and visibly relaxing. I became skilled in getting out of a door easily with a bucket and brush when a whole pack was trying to follow me. And, perhaps most importantly, I learnt that small sweet-looking terriers were much more likely to bite you than big scary-looking Dobermanns.

After the kennels and when my school days were over, I went on to study Zoology at university, a subject I loved and which allowed me to study animal behaviour and psychology with great scientists, such as the compassionate Professor Donald Broom. After a very short career in publishing, I was lucky enough to work for one of England's leading animal welfare charities, which had just moved its headquarters close to where I lived. It was there that my career in animal behaviour really started and took off. Eventually, I became Head of Animal Behaviour, the first of my kind in the rescue dog world.

The acquisition of all this knowledge and dog experience stood me in good stead for taking on rescue dogs of my own at a later date. I've had several throughout my life but the most testing, until Chesil, was a black Labrador/Weimeraner mix called Beau. He had bitten at least ten people that we knew of before I took him on, and was quite a challenge. As well as Beau,

Good credentials

I owned a rescue Springer called Sammy who was a perfect angel of a dog, loving and sweet to all she encountered and a good contrast to the more powerful and damaged Beau.

As well as these two, I raised a Rhodesian Ridgeback called Winnie from a puppy. Her only fault was that she chased cats – she no doubt found these a good substitute for the lions her ancestors were originally bred to chase. Although she never caught one, I didn't like her to scare them and worried that chasing one into the road would cause an accident. I once queued up at Crufts to ask the famous Barbara Woodhouse for a solution. She glared at me over the top of her spectacles, and said, 'Oh that's easy, my dear, you keep her on a lead'! She was right, of course, but I needed more and, eventually, I found a behaviourist, John Rogerson, who seemed to have all the answers. He had asked me if Winnie played with toys. When I said no, he told me I must have another dog at home. How did he know?! I was fascinated. After a longer conversation with him, I was hooked and so began a long voyage of discovery into the realms of animal behaviour.

My little pack taught me a lot as they grew and developed and I spent hours just watching them interact and play. After the last of my dogs died of old age and after 12 years of the exhausting fire-fighting work of rehabilitation, I left the charity. I was tired of putting emotionally broken dogs back together, which perhaps helps to explain why Chesil was such a difficult project for me to take on. Before I met Grant, I wanted to concentrate on a long-held dream of doing preventative work. My goal was to set up a network of puppy classes around the UK, and perhaps the world, so that everyone had somewhere to get good education to prevent their brand new puppy 'going wrong'.

I had recognized early on in my career that puppies didn't come with a manual and so I decided to write one (*The Perfect Puppy*, now in its second edition, has sold many thousands of copies worldwide), based on all the knowledge I gained from working with dogs that had been ejected from their families for bad behaviour. This sold well, but only reached people who would sit down and read a book. Also, although a book can give you the knowledge you need, it's not easy to learn the physical skills and techniques necessary for puppy training without a teacher, so puppy classes seemed the direction to head in.

With a network of well-trained, professional tutors, I knew we would be able, collectively, to help owners go down the right path with their puppies from the outset. I'd been running puppy classes in my spare time while working full time, so I knew how much fun and how rewarding it could be. Owners just starting out with a new puppy are keen to learn and really want to get it right. It made a refreshing change from the owners I worked with during the week who were already at the end of the line with their dogs. The young puppies that came to the classes were keen to learn and please their owners, so different from the untrained adolescent dogs I was used to dealing with at work. I thought that if I could reach people at the start of their relationship with a new pup, it would be so much easier to help them than to wait until they were already struggling and impatient with an older disobedient dog. So I started Puppy School, training tutors from around the country to run good-quality puppy classes using only positive, reward-based techniques. For the first few years, this took up every minute of the day and there was no spare time to have a dog in my life.

Eventually, I began to win the battle of wrestling the Puppy School octopus and it became successful and more self-sufficient. Some free time began to emerge and my heart had healed after the loss of my lovely old dogs. At first, I wasn't sure what to do but then the urge to get a puppy became almost overwhelming and Spider, my beautiful Beauceron, came into my life. I used all the knowledge I had gained over the years to raise him, dredging up all the ideas I frequently passed on to others, and knew the very best people to get advice from when things took small turns in the wrong direction during adolescence. Spider was raised only with positives. He did have to learn boundaries and that he couldn't have everything he wanted, but he was taught with love and kindness and a good deal of tasty treats. He had to grow up good as, after all, I was the founder of Puppy School, an organization set up to provide puppies with training for life-long good manners, and it would have looked very bad if I couldn't get my own puppy to behave. So I put in the effort necessary to ensure he turned out well.

Consequently, he was my perfect friend and accompanied me everywhere, showing off his favourite tricks and training skills with great enthusiasm. He even came with me to the board meetings when I became a Trustee of Battersea Dogs and Cats Home, running round the table, carrying his fluffy duck, looking for someone to take an interest in him whenever there was a break in proceedings. He was also my child substitute, receiving all the nurture and care that I would have given to children had my life taken a different turn and, dare I say, a bit of a mummy's boy. It was when Spider was four years old that I met Grant.

Grant is the antithesis of a mummy's boy! He is tough, resolute and nobody's fool. He believes dogs and men should go out together and hunt in the woods, not stay inside with your dog lying upside down on the sofa, head lolling. To be fair, Spider was very fit, running beside me when I rode my horse, keeping up at full gallop until one of them gave in and slowed down. But he was used to responding to quiet whispers of requests, not loud demands for obedience.

I made it clear from the outset that it was 'love me, love my dog' and, such was Grant's love for me that he learned to adapt. Little did I know then how soon I would have to return the favour! From the beginning, Grant learned that Spider had to be carefully considered before I would agree to go away on holiday and that dog-sitters had to be found because I would never leave him languishing in kennels.

Although there are reputable kennels, I knew that it was very difficult to find one. During my teenage years working in kennels I had witnessed, first hand, some very dodgy practice. The boarding dogs were housed in horse loose boxes, with four or five dogs spending their whole stay in one, sleeping in beds placed around the outside. They weren't let out or taken for walks, but the owners never knew as they weren't allowed down to visit. On the rare occasion they did make an appointment to see the kennels in advance of leaving their dogs, they were shown the top kennels, reserved for the breeding dogs, which had lovely runs and lots of room.

While appreciating that the loose box idea wasn't a great way to keep dogs, I reasoned that they were only there for a few weeks and at least they were safe and well fed. As a teenager, I had no power to change things, but I did my best to make the dogs as happy as possible whenever I was there.

As well as being aware of my thoughts on kennels, Grant learnt that even though Spider had a dog flap to get in and out to the garden, I was only willing to leave him alone for an absolute maximum of five hours, but never on two consecutive days. In addition, Spider had to sleep in the bedroom on his bed next to me as he had done since a puppy. He was a pampered pooch indeed, and his welfare was my top priority at all times. Considering Grant's rough-and-ready approach to dog ownership, this was quite a change for him. However, he coped well, managing to adapt his previously learnt behaviour around dogs remarkably quickly. Changing the rules he lived by, such as 'no dogs allowed in the bedrooms' must have been difficult for him but he didn't whine about it, preferring instead to humour me and allow me to continue as I pleased. When he moved into his new house with its pale green pristine carpet, we had joked about Grant finding Spider socks to wear to prevent him walking mud through, but they never materialized. He treated Spider kindly, and rapidly learnt the request words and hand gestures that I used for communication and direction. Although we didn't know it, these would be so useful at a later date when we acquired Chesil.

Grant and I had met about nine months before Chesil moved into sharp focus and, until then, we had led the idyllic existence of new love, all happy and exciting. I've always found it difficult to live in this world of humans and Grant somehow managed to calm my fears and give me the security and strength I needed to feel content. I was no longer awake at 4 am, worrying about anything and everything. If I woke up and started to fret, Grant would wake up too, talking to me and holding me tightly, soothing my concerns until I was calm enough to go back to sleep. After a while, I began to sleep soundly all night. I imagine the sense of safety that Grant gave me was similar to how I made my rescue dog Beau feel when he came to live with me, and I knew our relationship was likely to last forever. What I didn't know was that Chesil was about to burst into our happy and carefree days and turn life upside-down.

Chapter 3
The dilemma

GRANT and I had met at Easter and since that time he had frequently talked about 'his' dog, a dog he shared with his ex-wife but which, in reality, I never saw as he couldn't have her at his house while he was busy working long hours. The fact that she didn't travel well in the car was his reason for not inviting her over for the occasional weekend when his 16-year-old daughter, Holly, came to stay. So I heard a lot about Chesil but never saw her. In Grant's eyes, she was the most wonderful Chesapeake that ever walked the earth. He talked of her in glowing terms and frequently told me how lovely she was.

It was rare for someone to own a Chesapeake – I knew from my days working in rescue that they were not an easy dog for the average owner. I was impressed that Grant had sourced a good one and it had turned out well. Not only was he my perfect man, but he seemed to be some kind of wizard when it came to dogs, too. I was expecting to meet the sweet-natured, good-looking, well-behaved angel that I had seen through Grant's mind's-eye when he talked about her, and so nothing had prepared me for what greeted me on our first meeting.

It was late summer and Spider and I were enjoying the peace and quiet of the back garden of Grant's house. Then in burst Chesil... His ex-wife Diane had brought her over for a two-week stay while she and Holly went on holiday. Fortunately, Diane and I were well acquainted, and we seemed to get on well. I liked to listen to stories of Grant's past antics, told from a perspective that I would never, otherwise, have been privy to.

So when Diane arrived that day, my full focus was on Chesil and I was curious to meet the dog I had heard so much about. My first glimpse of her was as she erupted through the back door and into the garden, muzzled and fighting her lead, towing Diane in her wake. Chesil was large, sandy-coloured and slightly fluffy, but her overriding feature was her excess weight, which resulted in her skin being pulled tightly over her very fat back and sides, and made it hard for her to waddle, let alone run. I could see Diane was struggling to control Chesil so, as the garden was enclosed, I suggested she let her go. I sensed they would both be better off if they weren't tied to each other. Diane gave me a worried look and released her.

The dilemma

Chesil promptly squatted and did a large smelly pooh right in front of us, causing a flurry of scolding and mutterings as Grant rushed to clear it up. It was too late, though, and the smell lingered on for a long time afterwards. Then she urinated close to the outdoor table where we frequently ate breakfast, kicking up her back feet when she had finished as if proud of herself. She proceeded to waddle in a determined way around the garden, investigating everything and pushing herself into the bushes and delicate flowers, destroying all that was in her path.

When she was calmer, I let Spider go to meet her. I didn't worry about introducing dogs because as a teenager my work in the kennels had taught me how to read their body language and predict how they would act. In the terrible kennels where I had worked, dogs from different households were kept together. When there was a new arrival, we would have to put all the dogs on leads and bring in the newcomer to see if they would get on together. It took a certain skill to hold four dogs on a lead at once, never allowing them to get tangled, and being ready to haul one of them backwards if it looked as though it was squaring up for a fight. As risky as it seemed, we never had a serious fight or even any injuries that needed treatment. There would be lots of sniffing and investigating, but with so many dogs in such a small space, very few had the nerve to become really aggressive.

Although thoroughly stressful for the dogs involved, practices like this one taught me so much and I have never forgotten the lessons on how to watch for subtle signs to predict what they would do next. I learnt that tail and ears held high means that the dog is confident and may get into a fight if another dog is showing the same signs. Dogs that cower away, tail clamped down and ears back are okay if left alone, but may suddenly flare into an impressive threat display if pushed too far by another dog. Dogs that hold very still can go either way, deciding that they are safe and dropping into a play bow or suddenly growling or snapping at those that keep on with their advance. The easiest tend to be the young, well-socialized ones who approach dogs by wagging their tail, with their whole body relaxed, looking for friends and wanting to play.

I would hold the other dogs while the more experienced staff member brought in the newcomer. Sometimes the existing pack would growl and get pushy with the new dog, or the new dog would strut around, tail up and worried. I learnt which type of dog would make friends easily and play, and which needed to rush to a bed and curl up, staying there until it felt more confident. Since I paid attention to the dogs as I cleaned and fed them, feeling sorry for them in their prison and treating them like new friends, I knew their different personalities, and it wasn't long before I could accurately judge which group of dogs the new dogs would best fit in with.

Since I learnt so much from these practices, I could often tell in advance which dogs would be okay together and which meetings would result in a fight. Chesil was still muzzled from her car journey, a ploy I later learnt prevented her from ripping great chunks out of the back of the seats in her frenzy when she travelled. I also knew she had landed in another dog's territory and so was unlikely to start anything in case she couldn't finish it. Spider would investigate her, find out she was female and be accepting of having her on his patch.

They met nose to nose, weighing each other up. Spider sniffed her and they interacted for a while, but she was stiff and starchy and unable to make friends so Spider came back to sit with me. It was all a bit of a non-event. After the encounter, Chesil went over to where she had previously urinated, sniffed, then dropped her shoulder and rolled, wriggling her back so that her neck and shoulders got a good coating of her scent. It was less than delightful behaviour for a first meeting and I remember thinking, 'Thank goodness she's only staying for two weeks.'

The thought of living full time with Chesil was not one I wanted to contemplate. Unfortunately, no matter how much I loved Grant and despite his rosy view of her, once I got to know her, Chesil was, in my opinion, simply the most disgusting creature you could ever wish to meet. I don't think he had meant to misrepresent her to me, but he had viewed her in a way that was very different to reality. After two weeks of struggling with her, even he had to admit that she wasn't an easy dog live with. For me, this unlikeable dog was a big intrusion during that two-week stay, disrupting our lives, fighting with Spider over possessions, and causing much aggravation and annoyance to all. As far as I was concerned, Chesil was part of Grant's past and I wanted her to stay that way. I was so glad when she eventually went home.

Chesil had been bought as a puppy for Holly, their daughter, to replace a much-loved Chesapeake called Harvey who, ironically, had been rehomed to the family as a puppy by the charity where I worked. Sadly, he had died of meningitis at just a year old and was badly missed by all. Unfortunately for Chesil, she had arrived at a difficult time for the family. Shortly afterwards, Grant and Diane decided to separate, which meant less time and emotional energy to devote to Chesil's upbringing.

Without anyone to teach her how to be good, she acted on any impulse that felt appropriate at that moment and became very badly behaved as she grew older. This resulted in her living a very restricted life in the kitchen. She did have a big garden to run in and the kitchen and garden were connected so she had a lot of relative freedom, but what she really needed was company and attention and, without this, she ran wild and was lonely.

This changed when Diane and Holly moved house. At first they moved to a house where life was not much different for Chesil. By the time, a few years later, they moved to another small town house in the same area, walks were getting increasingly rare, largely because of Chesil's deteriorating behaviour towards other dogs. Since the kitchen in the new house was smaller, Chesil's life was now seriously restricted. For a young Chesapeake, with a big brain and a body bred for work, life in a small kitchen must have been a frustrating existence. Unfortunately for her, she was just considered to be naughty and difficult to live with and, although they loved her because she was part of the family, she wasn't an easy pet for them.

Without the exercise and mental stimulation a Chesapeake requires, it was impossible for Chesil to be anything other than naughty. She tried hard to make herself comfortable, either using up her excess energy to hunt for food and guard stolen packets, or jumping up and being a nuisance to try to get much-needed attention.

To make matters worse, she then developed cancer of the mouth. Although this was treated successfully, it left her without one of her lower canines. This allowed her tongue to, quite literally, fall out of her mouth if she didn't hold it in and left her with a fairly gormless expression when she wasn't concentrating. Holly did a great impression of Chesil, her tongue hanging out to one side and her eyes rolling, which made us all laugh. Later, we joked that, if we ever had enough money, we would have a titanium tooth fitted to hold her tongue in and to scare burglars when it glinted in the moonlight. In truth, she didn't need a titanium tooth to scare burglars.

It was soon after her two-week stay with us that Chesil's behavioural and aggression problems began to escalate. She had always been aggressive over food or any item she had taken. Chesapeakes readily choose the fight option if they find themselves under threat, rather than running away or trying to appease. This unappealing trait helps to explain their low numbers among the pet population. Chesil didn't know how to give things up without a fight in return for something safer or better, and, with dogs like this, the problem is made worse by scolding or chasing them around. Chesil was very confident about her ability to keep people away from things she wanted, and this had resulted in many frightening experiences for members of the household, including quite a few biting incidents.

Things came to a head in December when, after nearly a year of living in cramped conditions, Chesil began to step up her level of aggression. One evening

Chesil had been allowed into the living room. There was a terrifying incident as Diane bent down to put tea cups on the table. Chesil launched herself at her face ready to bite. Only the quick thinking of a visitor pushing Chesil aside saved a very nasty incident.

Chesil was herded back into the kitchen where she set about taking all the items off the kitchen surfaces that belonged to Diane and placing them neatly in her bed. Interestingly, she targeted only Diane's possessions and left Holly's and other household items where they were. When Diane came back into the room, Chesil was sitting on her bed, on top of Diane's possessions, growling and baring her teeth as if daring Diane to come and get them.

Quite why she had done this is unclear, but it wasn't the first time she had been aggressive with Diane. Chesil may have seen Diane as someone who she could bully to get her own way, or she may simply have been unnerved by the noise level and exuberance of the visitors. After the incident, it is likely that Chesil felt insecure, and so gathered about her items that smelt of the strongest of the humans in the household, as dogs are prone to do when they feel alone and threatened. When Diane opened the door, Chesil may have growled and showed her teeth in self-defence since both of them were feeling tense and worried about what might happen next.

As you might expect, whatever the reason for this behaviour, it was extremely frightening for Diane and she decided she could no longer keep Chesil. So while her future was decided, Chesil was put into kennels, and remained there for the next seven weeks.

The options were limited. Putting Chesil into the rescue system wasn't possible as, with her track record, no one in their right mind would want to take her on. She would face a very uncertain future, possibly being passed around a few homes before being put to sleep. When I had worked with rescue dogs, only a handful of Chesapeakes had been brought in, but all had been aggressive and as difficult as Chesil. I found them to be strong-willed and likely to choose aggression over backing down or trying to run. When these traits were combined with their physical strength and hard bite, it made them dangerous and all had been put to sleep rather than rehomed. It was possible that there was someone out there who was willing and able to rehabilitate Chesil, but a person with the knowledge and experience required would be hard to find. So that left only two possibilities: one was to take Chesil to the vet and have her euthanized, which, at four-and-a-half years old, seemed a terrible waste; or Grant could take her on and we could rehabilitate her between us.

When it was proposed that Chesil could come to live with us, my reaction was a very definite 'No way!' It is not often I dislike a dog. Having spent my whole life working with them and trying to make their lives better, I can usually find something to love about them, and tend to coo over puppies in the same way that most people coo over babies. But Chesil was different. After spending years working in rescue, rehabilitating dogs such as Chesil, I definitely had the knowledge and ability to do it, but was I willing to put myself, and Grant, out to do so? I knew, more than most, how much work it was going to require and that the work continued for as long as the dog lived. Someone once said that aggressive dogs are like recovering alcoholics; there is always potential for them to fall off the wagon. I knew that we would spend the rest of Chesil's life making sure circumstances were right to prevent her going wrong again. It was not the kind of responsibility I wanted.

I also knew the disruption she would cause to our happy existence for the first few years. Selfishly, this was really the last thing I wanted. I had done my time with problematic rescue dogs, helping thousands of them to a better life, and it had been extremely exhausting and draining. I had left that world with some sadness, but with lots of relief and no desire to return. I was now working with puppies, which was a lot easier – they are little clean slates on which to draw the perfect image of the dog you eventually want. Better still, new owners are very keen to get it right and to work hard to achieve the desired result. Rescue dogs with issues, in comparison, are someone else's problem, requiring a huge amount of time and energy. I wanted to devote that time and energy to Grant – to our new relationship and our future.

Unfortunately, the alternative wasn't much of an alternative for either of us: the fact was Chesil either came to live with us or she was euthanized. I'd witnessed many healthy dogs being put to sleep at rescue centres because their aggression meant a new owner could not be found and it would be too dangerous to place them in the community. No matter how necessary you consider it to be, you never get used to that gentle sigh of their last breath when they were so healthy just one minute before. You also never get over the anger you feel towards their previous owners. Or the disgust you feel towards breeders who breed so single-mindedly to produce dogs that look good in the show ring that they conveniently forget about the difficult genetic traits they are handing to unsuspecting owners when selling a puppy. These owners and breeders are never there when the dog is killed and leave it to caring rescue centre staff, or the veterinary profession, for whom it takes a terrible toll.

Owners often pass their problem dogs on to rescue centres having kidded themselves that their dog will be homed in an idyllic place, such as on a farm where it can happily live out the rest of its days. Those of us who have worked in rescue know that no such farms exist. Each day, many hundreds of dogs die at rescue centres and veterinary surgeries around the country because someone didn't take enough care or have enough knowledge to raise them well when they were young. Over the years, I had become hardened to this fact and learnt that I couldn't save them all, no matter how hard I tried. For me, whatever the reasons and however understandable they might be, Chesil would be just another one of the hundreds.

For Grant, however, with his personal connection to her past, Chesil would never be just another problem dog. He had taken her into his family and, as a man who took his responsibilities seriously, he felt that he should at least try to solve her problems. He was also rightly worried about the effect on his daughter, Holly, of deciding to put a dog she loved to sleep. His strong sense of responsibility and duty were things I loved about him so I couldn't just brush them aside when it suited me. Besides, he genuinely loved his errant dog. Quite why I couldn't imagine, but he did. He wouldn't have asked me to give up my dog for him, so how could I ask him to give up his dog to please me?

Time was passing while we deliberated, and the poor dog had already spent a very long time in kennels so something had to be done. For Grant it was unthinkable that a dog he had helped to buy as a puppy should be killed at just four-and-a-half years old for want of a home that he could provide. The fact that he worked full time and couldn't take her with him meant that she would have to spend all day in a kennel in the garden until he came home in the evening and, unlike my own opinions on this, he was prepared to do this rather than have her euthanized.

He was sensible enough not to let it become an issue between us and tried to see things from my point of view. If he had decided to take Chesil on regardless of how I felt, I may have dug my heels in or even walked away. How you handle small crises in the first year of a relationship is important and he made it into a joint decision that didn't force me to do it his way. This was a clever move on his part as I loved him for it and it allowed me time to view things from his perspective.

So, despite my misgivings, and after worrying about it for many days and nights, Chesil eventually came to live with us. At the time, I was living in my own house, so, technically, she went to live with Grant. He always assumed I would help with the rehabilitation, which indeed I did, but knowing I could go home at the end of the day and leave him to it if things got too much made me feel so much better. I could always walk away completely, leaving them both to their fate together and moving on to another life. Although I never got close to this decision, having the option gave me the freedom I needed not to choose it. I know this possibility also played on Grant's mind, although he was smart enough not to bring it up or encourage me to think about it. And there was always the ultimate option of a one-way trip to the vet. As awful as that was to contemplate, it was, at least, a way out for us all.

I wasn't sure, given Chesil's personality and problems that we would ever be able to put her right. For this reason, I refused to take photographs or keep a record of her rehabilitation as I would have done normally. As well as being a useful way to chart progress, it is useful evidence, professionally, when teaching others about rehabilitation. It is also very rewarding to see a dog improve and so it a good thing, on a personal level, to have 'before' and 'after' photographs. With such a close emotional connection to the family, it didn't seem right to take the 'before' photos of Chesil, just in case there was to be no 'after' in the future.

Chapter 4

Tale of the bunny skin

'LEAVE it, Chesil!' I yelled. I could see her in the distance, hunched over something she was chewing, using her strong back teeth to pound it into pieces, and swallowing down great chunks of it from time to time as I ran towards her. We were in the middle of a large field and I knew whatever she was eating would have been rejected by the foxes as, in late winter, little goes to waste in the countryside.

Since Grant didn't get home from work until late, I often volunteered to go to his house early to release Chesil from her kennel and take her for a walk while it was still daylight. It had been a few months since she had come to live with him and she was now used to being in her kennel during the day, even if it was for many hours with little to do. Grant would give her bones and, at my request, large strong toys stuffed with her food, together with a large ridged ball with pâté smeared into the crevices. It would take her hours to clean out the ball, keeping her entertained for quite a while, but, even so, it meant she spent many hours with nothing to do except sleep and wait. So I would feel sorry for her, and for Grant since walking the dog in the dark twice a day is not pleasant, and make a special effort to finish work early so I could drive over and spring Chesil from her prison.

Grant and I had taken to staying in most evenings since Chesil's arrival, instead of going out or visiting friends. I was with Spider all day and so leaving him in the evenings wasn't a problem. Chesil, however, was cooped up in a cage and so leaving her all evening too didn't seem fair. I slightly resented the end of our carefree existence, seeing it as a premature end to the most exciting phase of our relationship but, since it was winter and it was dark by the time Grant got home from work, we quickly settled into our quieter life without too much thought. For our evenings to be stress-free, Chesil had to get plenty of exercise so that she would want to lie down and rest, so it was worth making the extra effort to get over to Grant's house to walk her.

At this stage, Chesil and I had a very limited relationship. I didn't live with her and so, as far as she was concerned, I wasn't an important member of the family. Although I tolerated her, I didn't feel any abiding affection for her as Grant did. I was content to leave her for Grant to deal with, wherever possible, which meant that I avoided any encounters that might result in aggression. I knew it would take time to earn her respect, since she seemed to have very little for the previous women in her life. I was careful not to let her get away with any behaviour I didn't like but, apart from that, I left her to her own devices. Most of the time, we circled around Grant in our own orbits, keeping out of each other's way as much as possible.

I would walk Chesil through the village and over the fields away from the sheep and other dog walkers to a place where she couldn't get into too much trouble. The advantage was that, on a sunny day, there was a lovely view over the gently rolling Cotswold hills. In mid-winter, however, there were many days when it was cold and dull. Spider and I would walk with our heads down hunched against the wind and rain, while Chesil, freed at last from her cage, would race ahead, hunting in the hedges and chasing leaves or birds just for the thrill of doing it. To see her running with such joy helped to stop me thinking and worrying about all the work that was mounting up back at home in the office.

Being the type of dog that needs lots of exercise to burn off excess energy and feel content, even a long walk on a lead wasn't enough for Chesil and so I tried to find her places away from roads where she was safe to run free. This took me to remote areas where no one goes and where we only had wild birds for company. This was in sharp contrast to my previous walks around the village with Spider where I would meet and get to know the other villagers out walking their dogs. The arrival of Chesil had brought the days of getting to know the neighbours, and having leisurely chats over garden walls while walking the dog, to an abrupt end.

We had been working with Chesil on the recall technique for a few weeks and she was gradually learning. We used food as an incentive and reward because she still didn't know how to play with toys. She had learnt to play with toys as a puppy but this hadn't been developed as she grew older, which meant she would half-heartedly chase the toy if you threw it, and then race away with it if you tried to get it back, staying just out of reach or getting aggressive if you got too close. This one-sided game soon ended, so we were still reliant on using food, rather than an exciting game with a toy, to recall her.

Chesil was very interested in food, especially now she was on a diet, so she soon learnt that it was to her advantage to return when we called and would hurtle back to us even from long distances. We hadn't, however, yet practised recalls when she was distracted by other things or taught her to come back when there was something else she would rather be doing. This is advanced work and can only really be successful if toy play rather than food is used as a reward.

So letting Chesil off her lead gave me a certain amount of anxiety since she was, essentially, out of control. I knew from previous experiences how foolish it was to let a dog free when you have no way to stop it running at another dog or a person, and no way of catching up with it. I had once made this mistake when I was a teenager working at the kennels. I let a very valuable Irish Wolfhound stud dog run in the fields behind the kennels without permission because I felt sorry for him always being in his pen. He bounded around joyfully, but worrying that someone would catch me, I called him back after a few minutes. He turned and jogged away from me. I jogged after him, and he kept himself just in front. He didn't chase anything but he kept his gentle jogging up, just out of reach, for three miles before he tired and allowed me to catch him.

I didn't want to make such a mistake again, but keeping Chesil on her lead would have restricted her exercise, leaving her full of energy and much more likely to get into trouble when we returned home. In these quiet, remote fields where no one went, I thought it was worth the risk. These farmers' fields were very quiet because there was no footpath. Grant had assured me that since this was set-aside land where no crops were sowed, it was okay to walk there. I still had reservations and this heightened my anxiety further. It was for this reason, perhaps, that I yelled louder and more aggressively than I otherwise would have done when I saw Chesil eating something in the distance.

She was still chewing as I ran up to her, breathless now and panting from my run. As I went towards her, she proceeded to gulp down the rest of her prize, not wanting to lose it to the crazed, fretful woman that had just appeared. As it slid into her mouth, I could see what looked like the skin of a long-dead rabbit. I worried that it would make her ill, or get stuck in her guts, or, even worse, that it may have been poisoned by the farmer and left for unsuspecting foxes.

She looked up at me, licking her lips, with a triumphant grin and I felt my anger rising. My anxiety about being somewhere I shouldn't, the mad dash across the field and losing another round against this difficult dog made me furious. I ranted and raved inside but knew that any punishment given now was pointless. It wouldn't prevent her doing it again in future, even if it made me feel better, and was likely to damage our fragile relationship. So I clipped on her lead and headed for home, muttering obscenities at her under my breath until I felt better, but remaining annoyed all the way home.

When you rehabilitate a dog, you are always torn between normal, human responses and the way you should respond if you want the animal to progress. I knew a lot more about behaviour modification than the average owner, but it didn't stop me having very powerful emotional responses to Chesil's unwanted behaviour, sometimes ones that threatened to overwhelm my self-control. I still didn't like this dog much, even though I tried not to show it, and particularly not at times like these, and I still resented her intrusion in our lives, particularly when she didn't seem to be keeping up her side of the bargain.

Sometimes, when things were going well, I would feel proud of our little achievements and begin to think that maybe she was okay after all. At these times, she was a joint project, and we all felt good. Grant and I would congratulate ourselves on our small successes and they helped to strengthen the bond between us. At other times, when she did bad things, I would feel she had let us down, broken our trust, wasn't playing fair, even though I knew that dogs know nothing of such abstract concepts. I would be cross with Grant for taking her on and wish that I had been stronger in my attempts to keep her out of our family. I kept my feelings to myself, not wishing to upset him, but I fumed inside and fantasized about a life that didn't include her.

On this day, I had finished my work early, made the effort to go and release her, risked the wrath of the farmer to find somewhere safe to take her, risked letting her off so she could have a good run, and look how she had repaid me. I knew Chesil would not be aware that my bad mood was caused by her letting me down, but it didn't stop me feeling the emotion. In reality, she had just done what thousands of years of breeding had instinctively told her to do – grab waste food while you can as it may not be there tomorrow. She wasn't being naughty, she was just acting on instinct and didn't have all those complex ideas of guilt and appreciation that I wanted her to have. Deep down, below all the emotion she made me feel, I knew this and I struggled with myself to do the right thing.

Back in the safety of Grant's house, I sat down in the living room to recover from the experience and reflect on what had happened. The dogs were wandering around doing what dogs do when I heard retching. Immediately I was on my feet as Spider was trained to run to the back door when he felt sick. I would get there as fast as possible and he would hold long enough for me to unlock the door and let him outside. We were a team and it was a partnership that worked very well.

This time, however, it wasn't Spider, but Chesil. Acting on impulse like she always did, she didn't move anywhere and happened to be standing on the lovely cream rug in the living room. Within seconds a green and stinking half-chewed rabbit skin, with accompanying green drool and vomit was flooding over the cream rug, slowly invading the fibres and soaking into each one, making them all a delicate pale green colour and giving off a smell that was unbelievably bad. This time, even she could tell she had overstepped the mark and, once she had finished heaving, she shot out of the living room, running through the hall until she was under the kitchen table where she stayed until Grant came home. By that time, I was exhausted and grubby from frantically cleaning the rug as I'd raced against time to remove the last traces of green for when Grant returned.

I couldn't let Grant know how bad the whole sorry episode had made me feel or it would make him feel bad too. It was in his nature to want to take action to sort things out and there really was nothing he could do this time. So, as always, I knew I would tell him what had happened but keep my feelings, mostly, to myself, while fuming quietly inside and hating his horrible dog that was having such an adverse impact on our lives.

On Grant's arrival, Chesil came out to sit against his leg as I told him a toned-down version of the story. 'Have you been a bad dog, Chesil?' he said. Her ears went back slightly and her tail thumped against the floor as she caught the edge of scolding in his voice. 'She can't help it, she doesn't mean to be bad,' he said to me, faintly amused. She looked like a perfect angel and the very epitome of a good dog. Still frazzled from the horrible experience Chesil had just given me, I wondered if she would ever become the good dog that Grant thought she was and I wanted her to be. The rug in the living room would never be quite the same and, despite a later steam cleaning, always had a vague odour of rotten rabbit when you got close to it.

Chapter 5

Two steps back

CHESIL'S first few weeks in the house were characterized by mad dashes up and down the stairs, followed closely, if we weren't paying attention, by a puddle appearing on the landing. Being far too sensible to get caught in the act, Chesil would creep up while our backs were turned and leave a swampy patch of urine on the carpet at the top of the stairs. The placement varied, so it was unlikely that it was just a good place to relieve herself, especially since she would go outside to do so frequently.

She had been fully housetrained in her previous house. Clever dogs, like Chesil, are usually very clean. In fact, over the years I've noticed a direct correlation between cleanliness and intelligence. Once smart dogs know that the whole house is their nest, they are usually very reluctant to make it dirty and have a very clear distinction about what is right and wrong in the toileting department. Chesil was also clean in her kennel during the day, patiently waiting for eight or nine hours until she was let out to relieve herself, despite there being a concrete run where she could have gone.

I felt she was trying to make a statement by wetting on the landing. Quite what she was trying to state was open to interpretation. She could, for example, have been trying to make herself feel more secure by ensuring her new pad smelt like her, or she may have been trying to stake her claim to the upstairs rooms, having always been kept downstairs in her previous homes. Whatever her reason, it certainly had an effect – Grant and I were dismayed and then annoyed at having to constantly clean up these unwanted wet patches on the pristine carpet. They had to be soaked up with a paper towel, then scrubbed with biological washing powder solution, then rinsed, then dried, then wiped over with surgical spirit, if you could remember where the patch was by then.

Grant, in particular, was a stickler for cleanliness, and he was upset that she was using the carpet to urinate on, for no apparent reason. As the resident dog expert, he asked me for answers but I had none, only theories. I felt under pressure to solve the problem but before you can find a positive solution, you have to find the cause. It's easy if you are heavy-handed. Then all you have to do is lie in wait and heavily punish the next misdemeanour in the hope that it won't happen again, hoping that the fright and pain you cause in the process doesn't lead to any further behaviour problems. This wasn't my way of doing things and so we had to wait until I had more of an idea why it was happening.

In the early days when Chesil had only done it a few times, it was too soon to know the cause and come up with the solution Grant was desperate for. At this stage, I could only think of preventing it by keeping Chesil downstairs. We could have done this but she had led such a restricted life previously, and did so now during the day, that I wanted to give her freedom and try to find a way to stop the undesirable behaviour. I felt it was better, in all aspects of her life, to teach her how to behave well than to restrict her access to different parts of the house. Until I could identify a pattern, however, it was very difficult to know how to stop her urinating on the upstairs carpet, especially as she was sneaky and tended to do it behind our backs.

Sometimes Chesil would be good for days and then all of a sudden run upstairs and leave her trademark puddle. There is nothing quite like treading in warm dampness, feeling the wetness soak into your sock and ooze up between your toes as it slowly dawns on you what you are standing in. She would never do it anywhere else in the house, so there was definitely a reason for her wanting to urinate there.

Chesil had never been allowed upstairs in her previous home, and you could see her rejoicing in the freedom of being able to get onto the landing and into the bedrooms. Holly had her own room for when she came to stay and Chesil would often give that the once over, sniffing for any uneaten food left on a plate by a pre-occupied teenager. Grant would claim Chesil was 'looking for' Holly, and it was sad to inform him that, in reality, she knew very well that Holly was not there, but was, instead, on a far less noble mission to scavenge for anything Holly may have left behind.

When you take on a rescue dog, it always feels like you are taking one step forward and two steps back. Just when you think you are getting things sorted, there is a sudden backward slip for no obvious reason. We would just think she had overcome the wetting problem when she hadn't done it for a long time, then another wet patch would appear. It is very easy to become annoyed at such disruptive behaviour, rather than looking deeper for the cause. In reality, looking back, Chesil was probably just trying to make herself feel safer. By putting her scent at the very core of the house, perhaps this helped her to feel better.

Chesil had a way of happily bouncing down the stairs, tongue lolling, tail wagging. You could interpret this as happiness or, if you thought she had just left a puddle, satisfaction for a job well done. I took to racing up the stairs to search for wet patches when I saw this expression. Sometimes I would find nothing and be relieved; other times I would find a puddle and be incensed that she could be so sneaky, especially when she appeared to be delighted to have got away with it. Again, I knew that I was giving her far more powers of deceit and thoughtful planning than she possessed, but it didn't stop me being furious and, again, I had to wrestle with myself not to get cross with her.

After several such 'accidents', I realized that they often followed incidences where we had got upset with Chesil for behaving badly. Although we tried not to tell her off too much or scold her but, instead, find positive ways to teach her better behaviour, we were still disappointed at times and couldn't help giving her the cold shoulder while we got over the feelings of frustration. During these times, she would often sit on her bed with her face turned to the wall as if it was easier to hide than face us. This worried Grant as he had lost a dog to meningitis and the first symptoms had been for it to hide its head in the curtains. Chesil also developed stress lines on her face, long wrinkles appearing from the corners of her eye to the side of her face, and we knew she was in crisis when we saw these.

Social isolation is a powerfully unpleasant feeling for a social creature like the dog. If the 'crime' was very bad and we withdrew from Chesil for too long, she would feel the need to place another scent mark on the upstairs landing, the centre of her 'den'. Fortunately, thanks to our positive approach to her retraining, it didn't take long for Chesil to begin to feel happier and more secure and, as a result, the puddle incidents began to dry up.

I would have realized sooner that withdrawal of affection was causing the wetting problem if I had been looking at the big picture and not been so emotionally involved. It was difficult to be objective when I was caught up in the moment, especially when I would have preferred to be spending my time developing a romantic relationship with my new love, instead of rehabilitating his stinky dog. When Chesil came home from a walk yet again reeking of the fox faeces she had just rolled in, requiring yet another bath and taking yet more time out of our precious evening together, leaving us all with a faint, lingering, very unromantic smell, it was hard to sit down and think how we could help her to feel better about the world.

The one step forward/two steps back concept certainly held true for our experience of taking her for walks in the early months. She would behave impeccably for three or four walks, starting to respond to the recall cues we were teaching her, walking politely past walkers, sheep and other points of interest along the way. Then, for no apparent reason, we would have a disaster of a walk. She would growl at other dogs and we would have to haul her away on the lead, barking and growling ferociously, making us look like terrible owners; she would lunge at the sheep, nearly dislocating our shoulders and making us afraid for the day when we accidentally let go of the lead; and she would refuse to respond to our recall cues, defiantly sniffing a blade of grass or turning in the other direction when we called her.

It may have been that she was having a bad day and didn't feel well, or, more likely, that she had done something wrong early in the walk. In our despair, we withdrew our affection at these points and, as a result, she felt she could please herself and not respond to our requests. The lack of connection with us would make her more insecure and hence more likely to be aggressive in order to look after herself.

After a difficult walk with Chesil, we would hang our heads and wonder if it was ever going to be possible to rehabilitate such a difficult dog with such a delinquent history. We would feel hopeless and demoralized, which aren't good feelings when you are used to being successful and seeing little bits of progress every day. At these times, it was very natural for us to withdraw from her, feeling that we didn't want to be with her socially. And it was during these times that she was most likely to run upstairs and pee on the landing, enraging us further and widening the gap between us even more.

Despite how we felt, it was us who had to take the initiative to call a halt to this destructive divide between us. After all, we reasoned, we were the ones with complex brains and she shouldn't have to put up with us being difficult with her just because she hadn't learnt to behave well as a puppy. So we would have to forgive and forget, and try to rebuild our relationship with her again. It was usually me who suggested that we should reach out to Chesil to make her feel better. Grant was happy to ignore her and forget she was there for a while, after another particularly difficult episode. I would feel sorry for her much sooner, forgiving her more quickly and encouraging us both to do something with her that would enable us to reward and praise her. Once this occurred, her whole attitude would change. Instead of acting like a rebellious and spoilt teenager, she would begin to work with us once more, trying to please us and work out what we wanted of her.

The trouble was that when Chesil is upset, she doesn't act depressed or get sad. She has the sort of character that makes her tackle life head on, barging through difficulties, using shear brute strength to make things better. Grant has this type of character, too, but his is tempered by the rules and boundaries of social graces taught to him by his parents. Chesil had no such internal self-control and if she was upset, we all knew about it. She wasn't endearingly sad or sweetly put out; she was bad-tempered, aggressive and belligerent. These weren't endearing qualities and they caused us to withdraw from her even further. So it would take a monumental effort from us to take her back into the fold and work with her and her issues. I'm proud to say that we always found the strength, eventually, even if at times she felt our coolness towards her for a day or so while we regrouped. It wasn't long before we would find something she could be successful at so that we could be genuinely pleased with her again, and we could all relax and move forward.

The early days of owning Chesil were punctuated by difficulties and led us on an emotional rollercoaster ride that we couldn't get off. She was getting to know us, and we were getting to know her. It wasn't an easy process for any of us. More importantly, we were setting boundaries for acceptable behaviour. They weren't necessarily boundaries that she felt were appropriate and there were lots of times when she fought against them. We were resolute, however, and, eventually, being a social animal that finds it more comfortable to conform to the pack's social structure, Chesil thankfully began to behave in a way that we felt was more becoming to a pet dog.

Grant's natural instinct was to use intimidation to control and suppress Chesil's unwanted behaviour. With his deep, booming voice, he was good at it and when he shouted, Chesil reacted. But although he was good at stopping behaviour we didn't want, it wasn't teaching her much about how we wanted her to behave. Like any normal pet dog owner, Grant would usually ignore her when she was being good, satisfied that all was calm. This does nothing to teach or maintain the behaviour you are trying to encourage. Some social dogs, feeling they are being ignored, will, eventually, try behaving badly again just to get some attention.

So I tried to encourage Grant to show Chesil what he wanted her to do, and then praise and reward her for doing so. This is much kinder than being told off for doing something wrong. It was more work for Grant, though, who had to think ahead and teach good behaviour rather than just react when he was irritated; a tall order when he came home tired at the end of the day. And it was hard for me, too, to remember to remind him at an appropriate time, rather than just taking the short cut and doing it myself.

Once we began to do this – praising her for getting onto her bed, for being quiet when we had thought she might bark, or at any other time when we noticed she was being good – we started to make progress. We also actively worked at giving her things to do, such as going to her bed during mealtimes, and then praising her for doing so. I could see the relationship between Grant and Chesil becoming less 'me man, you dog, you do as I say' and slowly becoming 'we man and dog, we work together'. Chesil stopped being so worried when Grant approached her, wondering if she was going to be in trouble again, and, instead, started to look up at him expectantly, wondering what they were going to learn today.

I was impressed. Grant, like Chesil, is a fast learner and once he had got the hang of it, their relationship went from strength to strength. I used to wonder what would have happened if I hadn't been there to help. I suspect they would have rubbed along together, Chesil getting yelled at on quite a regular basis, but learning to accept it as many dogs do. She wouldn't really have learnt much, except to be worried by shouting humans. I saw this sort of situation with many of my clients. In the end, the loser is usually the dog, who has less power in the human-animal connection. I was pleased I had helped them to find a better path where they would both, in the long run, be happier.

Getting a good relationship with a pet dog is not easy. Some owners give their dog too much freedom, allowing it to run riot, setting no boundaries and letting the dog have too much of its own way. This sort of dog learns no self-control and is frequently shut away in another room or left at home because it is too disruptive for polite company. Other owners exert too much control, constantly being oppressive and dictatorial to get their own way and using threats and intimidation to force their dog to behave. Dogs that belong to tyrants are usually worried about getting it wrong and can learn to be defensively aggressive. They often live stressed lives and die young.

It doesn't have to be like this. Instead, good owners try to gently, but firmly, teach good manners and self-control. They set boundaries and ensure that their dogs do not cross the line, but they are quick to praise and reward good behaviour. These owners have the most positive relationships with their dogs and the best control. Their dogs genuinely want to please them and live in a household where they are not afraid to get it wrong or make mistakes. This creates a dog with a creative, exuberant personality that can be calm and well-behaved when appropriate.

Chesil had previously lived with owners who were very gentle with her, which allowed her too much freedom. Then, when she was naughty they had tried to be firm with her and had been unsuccessful. Because of this, setting boundaries and teaching her to keep within them wasn't easy at first and she fought against them. We didn't want to be oppressive, but we did want her to learn that she couldn't always get her own way and that, at times, she would need to give up what she wanted for the greater good of the family. We taught her this using praise and approval as a reward for compliance. This works well with social animals, but it wasn't easy when Chesil did something that upset and annoyed us, such as peeing on the landing. Then all our desire to be nice to her would disappear and she would run wild for a time before we got our emotional energy back.

I should have remembered the one step forward and two back phenomenon with rescue dogs, since I had been there and done that before with other dogs. The most difficult was Beau who was 18 months old when I took him on. He was already quite far down the path of knowing he could use aggression to get himself out of difficult situations. Underneath his bravado, he was a gentle soul, avoiding trouble when he could, but facing it head on if he thought it was necessary. He reminded me of myself and I sympathized with his problems, caused by a lack of socialization at a critical age and some harsh punishment for misdemeanours he didn't know he was committing.

My empathy with him helped considerably with his rehabilitation. When he trembled and shook, even though he was growling a warning at the same time, I understood his concerns and helped him move away from things he was scared of, finding time, later, to use treats and rewards to help him learn not to be afraid. Even so, I knew only too well that after a really good day when a breakthrough would happen and we would move forward, would come a terrible day where nothing seemed to go right. It takes a long time to get over fears and develop a relationship with the new humans in your life and, even though progress was being made steadily, bad habits took a long time to fade away, especially with a dog that had successfully used aggression over and over.

At first, Beau even scared me with his threat displays. He was large and black, with shiny white teeth that looked as if they were just waiting to sink themselves into your flesh. He had been out to two homes and had bitten people in both of them so his days on earth were numbered. I wasn't sure if I could rehabilitate him as he was aggressive to both dogs and people, but I knew I had to try. Taking the worst dog in the kennels and making him into a good pet would give me some much-needed respect for my work at a critical time in my career, as well as confidence in my own methods. So I gave it a try, taking great care not to get bitten in the process.

A few weeks after I took him on, I was walking him with my own dogs in the fields near to my house. My dogs were now used to him and I'd managed to introduce them gradually so that Beau became friends with them rather than enemies. Now we could walk together and, after so many months of being in kennels, Beau loved to run free. He was only 18 months old and in his prime, so when I let him off, he would run and run, keeping us in sight and catching us up just as we arrived back at the car.

As we walked one day, I became aware that he wasn't with us and so turned to look for him. He was standing still in the middle of a field, which was very unusual. I called him and he barked. I called again, and he barked again. Something was wrong. As I ran back to him, I noticed that he had got his front paw caught through the big chain that hung round his neck and was now completely stuck, one paw off the ground, chain cutting in behind his neck and behind his elbow. As he had a leather collar on that I used for his lead, I should have taken the chain off but his i.d. tags were attached to the chain and I had been too lazy to change them over. I had also left it on because I thought the brightness of the chain looked pretty against his dark fur.

Fortunately, I had grown up in the era of the check chain, a horrible device made of chain and worn like a collar that constricts tightly around the neck if the dog pulls on the lead. They were once common and many were too large, allowing the dog to do what Beau had done and put its front paw through the chain. As a result, I had released dogs from this type of predicament before. These had been friendly dogs and I'd been able to easily do the considerable amount of pulling and pushing required to free them. Whereas Beau had only been with me for two weeks and I hadn't got to the handling part of his rehabilitation yet, so I had no idea how he would respond to this. I couldn't lift him, however, and it was a long way back to the car, so I had no choice but to try.

So I began gingerly, pulling a little and letting go to see the response. Beau was a clever dog, as dogs that get into trouble with people often are. He seemed to know he needed my help and, as I got rougher, he tolerated everything I needed to do to ease him out of his situation. I had to take some big liberties, tugging and straining, trying not to hurt him, but fighting with the chain against bone and skin to get him out. He coped well, never once getting upset, and staying relaxed so it was easier for me to work with him. When we were finished and he was free, I felt we had bonded. From that day onwards, I was never afraid of what he might do to me, and he seemed to feel the same.

While getting him to be friendly with me was relatively easy, it took another two years of hard work before I eventually persuaded him that all other people and dogs were safe. We started out with colleagues at work, working with the bravest and gentlest people at first. We would get close to them, they would throw treats, I would praise him and we would move away before starting again, this time getting a little closer. Over time, he learnt to link the presence of people with positive things and, eventually, after much work and lots of handling exercises, he would go running up to people, body relaxed, tail wagging, happy to be with them.

One day at work, as we all sat having coffee together, one of the temps from the admin office sat stroking Beau, who was happily leaning against her. Something about him must have sparked a memory as she suddenly asked 'What happened to that awful black dog in the kennels that was so aggressive?' We all laughed.

'You are stroking him,' I said proudly.

Working with Beau's fear of other dogs was not so easy. While I could ask people who worked with him to do, and not do, certain things, it was not possible to control another dog that met him. Instead I had to carefully choose which dogs I put him with so I didn't scare him enough to send him back into his aggressive mode. This was relatively easy as there were plenty of dogs to choose from, owned by staff in the offices who were willing to walk with me and Beau while he overcame his fears. I worked hard on this, struggling through times when we would have relapses and he would lunge at other dogs, and gradually working towards a time when he was safe to be let off the lead.

Eventually, he calmed down and realized that other dogs were not out to get him as he had previously thought. He relaxed and learnt to trust my judgement on which dogs were okay and which were not. Since it was me, rather than him, that had grown up with other dogs, I could tell at a distance which approaching dogs would be trouble and which would be friendly. Beau's faith in my ability was strong and I could let him run free, safe in the knowledge that, should I need to call him, he would turn on a sixpence and race back to me, wanting his treats and fuss much more than he wanted to get into trouble with another dog.

Quite quickly, Beau and I became inseparable. Although I already had two dogs and didn't really want a third, I couldn't bring myself to put him through the trauma of finding another home with new owners. So, six months after I took him home for the first time, after signing some papers at work, he officially joined my family. Beau accompanied me to many of my UK talks and courses, working the audience to get as much fuss as possible. At the end, I would show them photos of how he behaved when I got him, to give them hope that they could make the necessary changes to their own dog or those of their clients. There was always a gasp as I showed a picture of him from the past with flashing, snarling teeth – especially if that day he had been happily rolling on the floor with the children.

We learned the sport of working trails together, and he became a Pet Assisted Therapy (PAT) dog, working as a doggy visitor in a local hospital for the elderly. One day, we found an elderly man alone in the conservatory part of the hospital and, before approaching, I asked if he would like Beau to visit. He indicated that he did and as he stroked Beau's head resting on his lap, he told me all about the black Labrador he used to own when he was younger. A nurse came in while we were there and looked startled. I assumed she didn't know about the PAT visit and was surprised to see a dog in the hospital. After our visit, we were walking out when she stopped me. She told me that the man we visited came into hospital regularly and was so upset at being there that he refused to speak. This was the first time in years that anyone had heard him talking. After that, we went back regularly to see him.

Beau lived a long and happy life with me until he died of a heart attack at the age of 13. He was the last of the three wonderful dogs I had owned as a young adult. As he lay unconscious in the back of my car while our kind vet administered his final injection, I looked at the sky, eyes full of tears and my own heart heavy, and wondered if I would ever be able to mend the wounds enough to own another dog.

Time heals and, eventually, one-and-a-half years later, I brought home my puppy Spider, happy to be a dog owner again and ready to risk the heartbreak that this would eventually bring. I was content with just one dog, never wanting to go back to the madness that comes with owning three at once. Taking Chesil on was still one dog too many in my opinion. One well-behaved dog gets invited to friends' houses, whereas you cannot expect them to put up with two. One well-behaved dog can be taken to the pub, even if he is large. Two dogs can create chaos and lead to disapproving looks from other people, especially if one is still in training. Chesil was far from well-behaved and she needed some serious training and rehabilitation before she was fit for polite society. For the moment, we usually left her at home when we went out, eventually realizing it was better to leave her behind and continue with a normal life than stay at home and slowly become more resentful of our loss of freedom. We took only Spider who we knew would not let us down in public.

It was during this phase of our lives with Chesil when I was at my house one day in the early evening, preparing dinner. We were having a much-needed evening away from Chesil as Grant was coming over to my place instead. It was quite like old times again, when we first started going out, before we had got bogged down in the drama of being 'parents' to Chesil. I had cleaned the house and got dressed up.

My home phone rang and it was Grant. 'I'm just out walking the dog, I'll be over soon,' he said. One of the things I loved about Grant was how communicative he was. You didn't haven't to guess what he was doing, thinking or feeling. He was happy to tell you, clearly and eloquently, at any time you asked, even at 4 am. His answers were so consistently positive about his feelings for me that, eventually, I no longer need to ask.

He often phoned when he got home from work and now that the evenings were getting a bit lighter, he would rush straight out with Chesil and call as soon as he got to a place where he could let her off. We continued to chat for a while when a loud 'Chesil, get away from that!' boomed down the phone. 'She's found a dead fox,' he managed to say hastily and I could hear him hurrying towards her. A deep rumbling growl began, so ominous that even I knew her intentions from many miles away. Some stamping and loud exclamations followed, and the rustlings of Grant's phone being held under his armpit to leave his hands free, and then I could tell they were in a stand-off. 'I'll ring you back,' said Grant and the phone clicked off.

I was left hanging, but I could imagine the scene. Man and dog had such a similar personality and neither would back down unless they really had to. No subtle ways of ending the disagreement, such as those I would suggest, were thought of or expected. It was a straightforward battle of wills. Grant would be standing over Chesil, threatening all sorts of unspeakable horrors if she didn't leave it and back up. Chesil would be hunched over the fox, growling and determined not to leave something she could have the pleasure of both eating and rolling in.

The minutes ticked by and then the phone rang again. 'Do you still have all your fingers?' I asked, half joking and half concerned.

'Yes, she gave up,' he said.

Only someone as strong-willed as Grant, with his prolonged eye contact, lack of fear and complete determination could take on a growling, focused Chesapeake and win, without needing to resort to a physical fight. 'I think she realized I wouldn't give in,' he said. Another round to threats and intimidation, although I had to admit it was useful with an untrained dog at times of crisis like this one.

Chapter 6

Sweating the small stuff

WITH a dog as complex as Chesil, I knew we would need to take things slowly to give her time to adjust to her new life. Rescue dogs take time to settle in and form relationships with their new owners. When Chesil first came to us, she had so many behavioural issues and bad manners that it was difficult to know what to tackle first. On a professional level, I have learnt to help with whatever the client has asked for advice on. Sometimes I'm asked to help with minor issues, such as jumping up, when it's been clear to me that there is a more severe aggression issue. I've learnt not to give advice that is not asked for, but have found you can gently lead owners to admitting they have more crucial problems with their dog. I've discovered that if you help them cure minor issues, such as jumping up, effectively and quickly, owners will then be brave enough to tackle more difficult behaviour.

Since I wasn't being asked for a professional treatment plan for Chesil, I didn't construct a formal rehabilitation programme but, instead, let it grow organically from our needs at the time. Our most pressing need was for a dog we could live with and so we decided to tackle her bad house manners first, before dealing with her aggression. For now, knowing that Chesil flew into an aggressive rage if you got near any chews, bones or toys she happened to have, we decided to only allow access to such things when she was alone and made sure that anything that could be stolen was kept well out of her reach.

Chesil's favourite place to run when she had something she needed to guard was under the kitchen table, which was placed against the wall, giving her a nice secure space, bounded by the chair legs on either side, which she could defend easily. If we were cooking and dropped a half-empty packet on the floor, she would be on it in an instant, grabbing the packet and then rushing under the table. If you heard the chair legs scraping loudly on the floor, you knew she had snatched something and had fled under the table at speed, pushing the chair legs out of the way in a desperate attempt to get to the back wall and safety. Frantic chewing sounds would then be heard and if you dared to look under the table, you would be greeted by snarling teeth and a deep rumbling growl that could be heard all through the house. She really meant it.

Grant dealt with this by moving a chair, and then tempting her out of the back door, conveniently situated next to the table, with some delicacy that was more delectable than whatever was in the packet. Once she left the packet under the table and was occupied with her new treat, he would jump back inside, shut the door and retrieve the packet. I took a more relaxed approach, preferring to leave her with it, accepting that what she had stolen was already lost. Her behaviour made us much more careful about what we dropped on the floor and, with us better trained, and with Chesil only having bones, chews and toys when no one was around, her worst problem – aggression – was put on hold. We then began to tackle easier things, such as teaching her good manners and the basic obedience cues that make life with a dog so much easier.

These cues are the ones we teach at Puppy School to puppies just starting out in life with their owners. They are easy things, like come when called, walk nicely on the lead without pulling, sit and lie down when asked, and to stay put until you are asked to move. They provide a good foundation of communication between dog and owner and allow everyday life to happen with the minimum of difficulty on either side. It is much easier to teach very young pups before they have learnt bad habits, but dogs of all ages can be trained. It just takes a little longer and a bit more patience.

Chesil knew very few words and even less about how to comply with requests, so it was going to be a long process to get her to respond in a way that would make life easy for us.

Chesapeakes are not easy dogs to raise and train unless you really know what you are doing. They were bred for duck-hunting on frozen lakes in the USA. They are rough, tough hunting dogs and one claim is that they will routinely retrieve 200 ducks in one day through the rough freezing waters of Chesapeake Bay. Dogs such as this, with their persistence, strong will, and high drive to work and exercise are not going to find it easy to fit into a home as a pet unless the owners have lots of interest in finding an outlet for their need to be active.

Their strong will, essential for the courage and determination to swim miles in choppy water to retrieve possessions, is extreme when compared to other dog breeds, and makes them very resistant to being coerced into doing something they don't want to do. They are not the sort of dog that you can force into cooperating with you, in the same way you can make a more sweet-natured breed submit to your will. Trying to make them do something against their will is guaranteed to end in failure. They will not be pushed and will resist, if necessary, resorting to aggression if you are too unpleasant with your insistence. Plenty of old-school gun dog trainers who use harsh methods prefer breeds like the Labrador, which can be coerced and bullied into submission. Chesapeakes take a very dim view of being treated in such a way and, rather than be cowed by such behaviour, will take action and become aggressive to stop the abuse if necessary.

Fortunately, using positive methods with Chesapeakes wins the day as they are very interested in learning how to do something that benefits them. This means you always have to work hard at first to find an incentive for them to behave well, until you have built a good relationship. I had spent years learning how to use positive reinforcement and had learnt first-hand, with my big black dog with white teeth and an aggression problem, how to gently work towards getting good behaviour on a daily basis. Since Beau had already learnt to defend himself, there was no margin for error. I knew I had to always keep control of myself and not resort to force and intimidation no matter how frustrated I was that I couldn't get him to comply.

About a year into the ownership of Beau, I taught him to jump a 3-ft hurdle so that we could compete in working trials. He was strong and agile and learnt quickly that touching the pole would make it fall down; he would sit patiently on the other side waiting for his ball to be thrown. One day, on a whim, I took the pole off and asked him to jump it with me holding it by one end. I gave the cue but he didn't move. I asked again, lowering the pole to nearly ground level this time. He didn't move again. I tried luring him across with food, but it wasn't a big enough incentive.

Finally, frustrated that he wouldn't do something he could do really easily, I shouted the cue at him, forcing him to do it rather than face my disapproval. This time he did, but as he did so, he closed his eyes and let out a long, drawn-out yelp. I realized at once that his reluctance was not because he didn't want to jump, but because he was threatened by me holding the pole. Someone had beaten him with a stick in the past and, even though we had a really good relationship, the sight of me holding what he thought was a stick must have brought back terrible memories.

In a second I was on my knees, the pole thrown aside, reassuring him and letting him know it was all right. I felt terrible and it was a good lesson for me not to resort to punitive measures to get my own way. Usually dogs have a good reason for not doing something and it is much better to find out what it is than to override their reasons and carry on regardless. After that, we worked with the pole and things that resembled sticks, pairing them with toys and food so that he learnt good associations instead. Eventually, I could bring a stick down from above my head, making a whistle as it cut through the air, and Beau would stand relaxed and wagging his tail, waiting for a game or some tasty treat, all thoughts of his previous bad treatment banished to a far corner of his mind.

Rehabilitating Beau was good discipline for me. My childhood had left me with a legacy of how to get angry to get your own way. I had rebelled against this, both at the time and later, and had actively sort out positive ways to get compliance instead. Beau was a dog that didn't allow me to forget my new ways, even for a moment, and I was grateful to him for making me work at these methods, refining and polishing them in a way that I may not have done without him. Since I had already learnt and used positive techniques, it was easy to transfer them to my work with Chesil.

One of my pet hates is a rude dog that dashes through the door ahead of me as soon as I open it, knocking me and whatever I am carrying aside as it races past. I don't really mind who goes first, as long as both parties are polite and cooperative about it, rather than one pushing and knocking the other out of the way to be first. Chesil was particularly good at this, using her excess weight to hurl herself into the tiny space between the doorframe and the door as it began to open, pushing the door into your face or slamming it back against the wall with a loud crash if it slipped past your fingers.

There were many occasions when we didn't want her to leave a room, such as when she was smelly from a good rolling session outside and awaiting a bath, or even when we just wanted a rest from being with her, which happened often in the early days. When visitors arrived at the door, she would rush to guard the territory, barking furiously. This is normal for visitors who have friends with dogs, but they expect it to end quickly once the owner gains control. Hearing a prolonged sequence of muffled thuds, growls, shouts and barking as the dog is herded into the kitchen is unnerving, especially if they were meeting Chesil for the first time. A hand grabbing her collar to haul her to the kitchen quickly was likely to get bitten and it wasn't a good idea to just open the door and let the visitors take their chances, so we tried to plan in advance for guests. At these times, we would keep her in the kitchen and, when the doorbell rang, we would have to squeeze past her to leave her there while we answered the door. Having been left regularly in her previous home for hours on end with no company, she knew that letting humans get out without her was not a good idea and so did her utmost to get out with them.

Years of practice of working with dogs in kennels had honed my skills at this manoeuvre, but this wasn't the case for Grant. On top of this, he has a very broad chest and so has to open a door fairly widely to get through it, leaving more than enough space for Chesil to exit too. So this method didn't work well for him and the situation would frequently arise where he was stuck in the doorway, trying to block a determined dog from forcing her way through with his legs, while shouting at her to back up. I would try not to laugh as I rescued him, holding Chesil back until he was through and then leaving her behind as I squeezed through. She was determined and strong and it took all my skill to manage it.

Teaching Chesil not to barge was, as it happened, relatively straightforward. I would open the door a fraction, she would shoot forward, and, before she got there, I would close it. After several attempts, the exhaustion caused by heaving her huge frame forward and back would leave her breathless and she would begin to hang back as the door opened, knowing there wasn't a chance she could get there in time. I would then be through like a whippet on the next opening, leaving the door open for her to follow when she was ready. Repeated regularly, she soon learnt that we were masters at this game and became resigned to waiting for us to go through without her.

As well as teaching Chesil not to barge past us, she also needed to learn that if she complied with our request to go into the garden or stay in the kitchen, she would not be left for a long time. By the time we had taught her to reliably 'sit' and 'wait', she had learnt to be more accepting about being by herself. She began to learn that we would always give her plenty of attention, and so she gradually became less desperate about being left alone and began to relax and take turns nicely at the door.

One of the difficulties I had was that I wasn't only rehabilitating Chesil, but also teaching Grant how to do it. This was far more difficult and time-consuming. We had formed a loving, equal partnership in our everyday lives but, suddenly, I had to be his teacher and quite persistent and controlling to make the lessons sink in. There were plenty of times when there was a conflict between social niceties and what would be best for dog-training purposes, such as when we were deep in conversation about something we enjoyed and I would notice that Chesil was about to roll in something unmentionable, or when I had corrected a technique but he was still doing it wrong and I had to correct him again. Knowing that, when rehabilitating a dog, letting it practise bad behaviour sets you back many days, I would always put Chesil's needs first, even if Grant was tired of lessons and being told what to do.

I tried hard not to keep on at Grant too much and he tried hard to remember I was trying to help and, somehow, we muddled through without fighting too much between ourselves. It was an unwelcome job at a time when we should have been cementing our love with happy, relaxing experiences and I was again resentful that Chesil's rehabilitation had robbed us of some of the delights of our first year together. Sometimes I would get annoyed at Grant's inability to do even the most straightforward of things concerning Chesil without being told and I would snap at him, making him annoyed and frustrated. He would then explain, in a dejected way, that he didn't have my skill or knowledge from years of working with dogs and that what was second-nature to me wasn't for him. This made me more cross as it stressed a difference between us, but I could see what he meant, and feeling sorry about the way I'd behaved, I would show him, again, how to get it right.

At times like this, I would remember just how much better I am at training dogs than people. Despite this, Grant managed to overcome my lack of abilities with humans and began to learn fast, showing Chesil what to do and practising hard to get it right. I began to realize that whatever I taught him, he would do. I just had to teach him everything as if he were a complete novice with dogs, and all would be well, so this is what I set about trying to do. I think it helped that we were in the early stages of our relationship, when we were both still trying to impress each other, and before we had reached the stage where we would start to take each other for granted a little. Fortunately, Grant learnt fast and picked things up quickly, long before my patience with man and dog wore thin.

One of the things he was not so good at was being consistent about not allowing Chesil to jump up. The breeder had told the family that 'Chesapeakes like to cuddle', by which she meant stand on their hind legs, with their front paws on a person and be fussed – so they had taken this to mean that it was important to allow Chesil to do this. Unfortunately, this is how everyone had greeted Chesil so, when we came home, she would rush to us and leap up, scratching at us with her front paws and pushing herself onto us until we responded. Since no one dared get near to her claws to cut them, her long, sharp nails dug in, leaving red marks on our skin beneath our clothes.

Sadly for Chesil, the family had sometimes tolerated this behaviour and then, at other times when they were in good clothes, they hadn't, and she would be pushed away and scolded. These inconsistent responses added to her arousal levels when she saw someone and made her even more frantic in her attempts to be accepted.

For me, jumping up is very unacceptable behaviour for dogs since it is a very unwelcome intrusion for most visitors and even more of a problem when the dog has muddy paws. A large dog might push someone over, especially a child or elderly person, and frighten those who are not sure about dogs. From the moment I got Spider, I had made sure he had never been rewarded for jumping up, bending down to greet him so that my face came to him rather than the other way round. When visitors arrived, I would tuck my thumb in his collar so I was ready to prevent any jumping and would ask visitors to greet him only when he was relaxed with all four feet on the floor. This worked well and, by the time he was six months old, he wouldn't even think of jumping up to say hello.

Now I was faced with this frantic dog scratching and clawing when I came to visit Grant and something had to be done. One of the most important things was to change Grant's approach, so that he didn't cuddle her when she greeted him in casual clothes and then hop around the kitchen, scolding and trying to avoid her when he was wearing his suit. Mixed messages like this confuse dogs and it takes longer for them to learn. For a smooth passage into the world of not jumping up, Grant needed to be consistent so that Chesil could learn that is was never acceptable to put your paws on humans.

Grant had grown up with dogs as a child, but relations with these dogs were always a little strained. There were Collies on the farm outside, but they didn't tolerate little boys and Grant learnt to stay well clear of them. Similarly, his mother's tiny Yorkshire Terrier had not appreciated the intrusion of the children and would snarl and bite if they got too close.

My response to dogs was very different to Grant's because, in contrast, my childhood experiences with dogs had been full of fun, love and trust. My family had always owned a dog and that dog had lived with us in the house. The first, which I hardly remember, was Jimmy, a Labrador-cross with a feisty temper. We were warned to stay away from his bed, where he would lay watchful, ready to growl if someone came too close. One day my sister was riding her bike past him as he lay in the hall. She was very young and wobbled at the wrong moment, sending her crashing onto Jimmy as he lay in his bed. My mother held her breath but Jimmy leapt out of the bed and didn't hold it against my sister, probably recognizing that it was an accident and not a deliberate attempt to gain access to his territory.

The next was Lassie, a black-and-tan mongrel, who was with us until she died of cancer at the age of seven. She was my mother's dog and was patient and sweet with us, putting up with us dressing her up and including her in our games. After a short gap, during which I pestered my parents constantly, we finally got a new puppy when I was aged ten, a small black mongrel called Scampi. She became my constant companion and I loved her dearly. My mother was terrified of us getting abducted by strangers and so discouraged me from going out to play with other children. Instead, I spent much of my time with my dog and rabbit, reading my books of animal stories and thereby learning all about animals, but little about how to interact with humans.

Despite having dogs of my own, I would regularly bring back dogs from the park that walked home with us and beg to be allowed to keep them. My wish was never granted and I would have to take them back to the park so they could find their way home. In those days, many people simply let their dog out of the house during the day, letting it back in when they got home in the evening. During the day, these dogs simply wandered around, forming small packs and taking themselves for walks. They were sociable and no trouble to anyone. Even though we lived in a semi-rural area, they didn't seem to bother livestock, and they learnt how to keep out of the way of cars or people that didn't like them. They provided plenty of opportunity for a lonely child like me to find new friends, which is why I was so desperate to keep the ones that had wandered home with me.

So my childhood experiences with dogs were very different to Grant's and our adult behaviour towards them reflected this. When Grant greeted dogs, they would get a brief pat and 'hello'. They would then be expected to go away and behave while he got on with other things. When I came home, I would be as ecstatic to see my dog as he was to see me and we would have a prolonged greeting with lots of exchange of love and affection. I could see that Chesil really needed this, especially in the early days when she was so unsure of herself, and so I made an effort to give her as much attention as she needed. Grant wasn't interested in prolonged hellos and his brief acknowledgement of Chesil made her even more frantic.

Interestingly, a similar situation arose with me a bit later in our relationship when Grant became so preoccupied with something he was doing on his computer that he thought a quick 'hello' to me would be sufficient when I came home after a long day. He wasn't exactly taking me for granted, but our relationship had now moved on from the need for exaggerated greetings and reassurances. He had, however, obviously moved on further than me and I was still in need of appreciation and enthusiasm when I arrived home. Much banging of pots and pans in the kitchen and slamming of doors later helped him realize that all was not well. Being a quick learner, he found out that, just like my dog, I needed to be greeted with lots of attention and affection if I was to go away and behave well while he got on with other things.

The way you greet a dog when it approaches you is only half of the story. Timing is critical for a dog that jumps up since it's important to reward the behaviour you do want (that is, all feet on the floor) and not the behaviour you don't want (that is, two paws on you). From now on, I decreed that Chesil would not be greeted or cuddled unless all four of her feet were on the ground rather than on people. We would simply ignore her and turn away so that she slid off and landed on the floor. Then, once all four of her paws were firmly on the ground, we would greet her like she was a long-lost pet that had trekked 1,000 miles to find us. This method does work well. I practised it consistently so that, for me, she stopped trying to jump up after just a few days, knowing that I would bend down to greet her instead. At first I had to be quick to reward the behaviour I wanted but, gradually, after a few weeks, once she realized that she wouldn't be ignored and that I would greet her soon after my arrival, even if not immediately, she began to relax and wait until I was ready to say hello.

Grant was very good at doing this for the first few weeks, even if he struggled to get it right in the beginning. His timing wasn't so good at first and he would forget to greet Chesil immediately. As he turned away from her and she slid off, something else would often catch his eye, like a pile of post on the side waiting to be opened and he would move over to do that instead of remembering to reward her. He would also turn too slowly or not move away, so that she would remain upright. I had underestimated the Chesapeake's amazing ability to stand up easily on its hind legs, front paws waving gently in the breeze as if it were meant to walk on two legs. When Grant turned slowly, Chesil would just wait, one front paw resting so lightly on his back that he wouldn't know she was there. When he turned round, looking down to see if she had landed and could be rewarded, he found himself nose to nose with her, eyes bulging in excitement, unable to contain her enthusiasm at getting so close to his face. We persevered, however, and slowly Chesil began to improve.

After the initial effort and concentration of the first few weeks, Grant began to slip back into saying hello when Chesil was up instead of down. Even though she didn't leap on us as much now, I was hoping to stop this behaviour completely whereas Grant was happy to simply stop the full assault when he came in the door. Worse still, there were moments when I came downstairs, still sleepy in the morning, padding down quietly in bare feet, to find them 'cuddling' in the kitchen, Chesil on her back legs cuddled in close to him in a state of bliss, Grant telling her what a good dog she was! Deciding that our relationship was more important than perfect behaviour from Chesil, I let this go, keeping up my own rigorous ideals so that she learnt never to jump up at me, but allowing Grant's inconsistencies. After all, she was his dog and this particular problem behaviour was never going to be a matter of life or death in our house.

Something that was more serious, however, was the biting of hands that held her collar. She wasn't fussy, any hands would do. Although she had never actually bitten anyone hard enough to break the skin, she would hold a hand in her vice-like jaws with ever-increasing pressure until the person was forced to let go. This made it difficult if you needed to move her away from something she had stolen, or into another room.

During my work with rescue dogs, I've come across many that were afraid to be held by the collar. Many owners will punish a dog by dragging it to the scene of the crime and then smacking it or rubbing its nose in a place where it has previously toileted. Puppies learn fast that it's not a good idea to let someone grab your collar, especially when that person is angry. Such dogs often grow up to be very worried about approaching hands and will snap or bite defensively.

Chesil hadn't been punished or had anything nasty done to her, but she had been forced to live in the kitchen. Since her behaviour in the house was so bad, it was easier to leave her there. It must have been almost unbearable for a social dog like Chesil to be away from the people she loved and cared about. A hand on her collar prevented her from getting through to the rest of the house, or perhaps from a packet containing food, and she had learnt to resent and resist.

I tried the two-handed approach to holding on that I'd learnt when I worked in the kennels, which was to hold on as long as possible and then to switch hands at the last minute when the biting became too painful. Although I wouldn't have recommended it to clients professionally as you have to know just when to let go, it worked quite well until Chesil got wise to it and started to snap at the approaching hand. She is a fast learner and I didn't want her to think that people could be kept away from her collar by an aggressive outburst. Also, I knew that Grant would find this approach more difficult. His usual way of dealing with her was to have a battle of wills to get her to move into the place of his choice. This did work, but involved a long stand-off with lots of threats and shouting, so was not an ideal method either.

So for this reason, and also because her aggression towards me was still quite unpredictable, I decided we would use a house line when we were all at home together. A house line is just a long lead without a handle that is clipped to the collar and drags around after the dog. The end can then be quickly picked up, giving you complete control should you need it at any time. You have to be careful not to stand on it if you are walking around together and a few funny incidents occurred when Spider had his feet whisked out from under him as Chesil sped past on her way to bark at something in the garden. Even Spider quickly learnt to avoid standing on her line.

This line, when we remembered to put it on, was a great bonus for leading her into places we wanted her to be or away from things we didn't want her to have. This was especially true when visitors knocked on the door. Amid the explosion of barking, we could pick up the line and get control of Chesil, quietly requesting that both dogs came into the kitchen while we answered the door. It was an offer Chesil simply couldn't refuse and she soon learnt what she had to do when people came to the door. It was certainly a lot better for my professional reputation than visitors listening to ominous noises from behind the door for several minutes as we hustled Chesil back into the kitchen without a line.

The house line was also useful for Chesil's bad habit of drinking out of cups or taking food off plates that had been left on low tables. This was an established habit for her and she would tour the downstairs rooms of the house, searching the kitchen surfaces, then moving onto the sitting room and dining rooms. She often raced in from outside, leaving muddy footprints with her front feet as she surfed the kitchen counter. She never missed anything and it was exceedingly annoying to come back into the sitting room, having popped into the kitchen to fetch a magazine, to see Chesil's tongue lapping at a recently made cup of tea. Even if you caught her just as she was lapping for the first time, it was too late. Some dog saliva was transferred and you would just have to go out, clean your cup really well, and start again.

I'm a fast learner, too, and I quickly realized it was easier to pick up Chesil's line and take her with me if I had to go out and leave food or drink alone. I rapidly became tidier, taking out my empty plates or cups immediately rather than leaving them for later, and never, ever, leaving things on the kitchen surfaces. Grant was already tidy, taking things out and washing them up straight way so, eventually, Chesil learnt there was just no point in looking. Besides, we were about to teach her that there was a different, more satisfying way to feel content rather than constantly searching for food.

Chapter 7

Light at the end of the tunnel

CHESIL lay on her bed, her body hunched around a small yellow duck toy that she was protecting. She was attached to me by my extra-long training lead and each time I pulled on it, an angry roar of protest came from her stiffened body. I could just see the whites of her eyes and teeth as she snarled and fought to control her prize.

Chesil had been with us for two months now and it was time to teach her that there was no need to guard possessions. We had come quite a long way in other aspects of life with her, and had made reasonable progress with her training and house manners. She was still very much Grant's dog, a fairly malevolent presence in his house as far as I was concerned. I still longed for the old days when it was just Grant, me and easy-going, well-behaved Spider. The relationship between Grant and me had changed slightly in those two months. We were now playing the role of parents to a troubled creature that needed our constant attention and it detracted from the previously idyllic existence we had once shared. That life was now well and truly behind us and I had no choice but to put up with Chesil so, wishing to make the most of a bad job, I knew that I would have to begin tackling the real issues, particularly her aggression, most of which were linked to her possessiveness.

So the long process of teaching her that people come to give, not take, began. We needed to let her know that we didn't want her yellow fluffy duck and that if we took it, we would give it back. There was no need for her to guard it from us and definitely no need to bite us if we came near. If Chesil was given a toy or found something she wanted to keep, such as a piece of stick or even a pen, and then brought it into the sitting room where we were, the whole atmosphere would change. Grant and I would become still and stop talking, Chesil would stalk about the room as if daring anyone to take it, watching us and alternately getting closer and then moving away as if to taunt us with it. Spider would move closer to me, probably to make sure I was protected, and watch intently. If either of us got up or began to approach her, she would begin a deep rumbling growl that was both menacing and frightening.

If we kept still, she would eventually go and lay on her bed with her trophy, growling whenever anyone moved. Eventually, one of us would have to sidle out of the door slowly, go into the kitchen and rattle a box of biscuits, at which point Chesil would rush out, all thoughts of her possession forgotten, leaving the other person to raid her bed and snatch up the object before she returned.

Obviously this state of affairs couldn't continue. My first idea was to put her on a long line, give her a toy and then bring her towards me. The theory was that bringing her into my space would calm her as she would now be on my territory. I could then carefully remove the toy, reward her with a treat, then give the toy back so that she would learn it was worth giving up her toy next time. I had done this before with less confident dogs than Chesil and it worked perfectly. They would come up, still wanting to keep their toy but a little less confident now, and I would wait just long enough until I saw signs that they were getting bored with holding it. A tasty treat produced at the right time would release the toy into a carefully placed hand and the toy would be thrown for them to chase. After a while, resistance on approach would fade and, eventually, the dog would realize that it was good fun and there was a high payout for taking the toy to the human. Having managed aggressive dogs often in the past, I thought I could do it without getting bitten and was willing to take the risk, although this technique should only be attempted by someone trained in handling dogs and is not something I would recommend to anyone else to try.

I carefully pulled on the line and, as expected, Chesil exploded into aggression and fought like a fish being reeled in. She thrashed and squirmed, being careful all the time not to drop her precious toy, growling through clenched teeth and a mouth filled with fluffy duck. To minimize the stress to her, and to Grant, I decided to speed things up and pulled her in quickly. The look on Grant's face as she flashed passed him told me that he didn't think this was a good idea. Grant trusted my expertise with dogs and usually accepted my suggestions for tackling Chesil's problems, but this time I could tell he was uncomfortable with the approach I was taking. Grant likes to do things safely. To him, reeling in a fighting, thrashing, snarling Chesil, with her eyes glowing red, didn't seem safe at all and I could see he was worried for me. Despite his misgivings, I felt I couldn't stop now and had to see this action through to its conclusion to teach them both that there was nothing to be worried about.

As Chesil came closer, she looked directly at me. It is rare for dogs in this predicament to have the confidence to do so and I have to admit it was unnerving, but I'm not one to give up easily and I knew that I would never recover my position if I backed down now. So I persevered and brought her right up so that her head was now on my lap. And I waited. And she waited, stiff as a board, jaws tightly clamped. Many minutes passed but, eventually, I saw her begin to soften slightly. Unfortunately, I was holding the line awkwardly and at this point I had to reposition, bringing renewed growling and more entrenchment. In this state of high arousal, she was very dangerous and my hands were very near to her teeth. Staying safe with aggressive dogs is more about knowing what not to do and I knew that any movement from me would prompt a bite, so I kept very still. There was nothing to do but wait for her to change her attitude.

While this stand-off continued, Grant had relaxed slightly and gone back to watching his programme, clearly accepting it was best not to get involved. Eventually, I noticed Chesil softening again, at which point I slowly produced a food treat from the bag behind me and held it above her head. She sniffed it, loosened her jaws on the toy, then clamped them shut as she realized she was losing her grip. She was a smart dog and not about to be fooled by that trick.

So I waited longer, for her arousal level to fall and for her to get bored with standing with her head over my lap. Patience is everything in situations like this, so I just had to wait it out. The next time, she decided the food was more interesting, and reluctantly let go of her yellow fluffy duck to take it. Before giving it to her, I lured her away from my lap until I could take the toy, out of her sight, with my other hand. She snapped up the treat and I grabbed the duck and threw it for her. She ran and grabbed it and leapt back in her bed. That was enough for one evening. I had learnt, over many years of dog training, to quit while you're ahead and not to continue to try to repeat your success over and over until the dog is tired and gets it wrong. Besides, I could see that Grant had also had enough of that type of entertainment for one evening. I went outside to rattle the box of biscuits.

Dealing with aggressive dogs wasn't new to me, but it still caused me anxiety. I'd tackled these sorts of problems with many different dogs for most of my life, and, each time, my heart would race and I would feel the same sense of elation when I survived the encounter with all my limbs intact. I'd started very young, while working at the kennels and dealt with some of the boarding dogs whose temperaments were less than perfect. I remember one dog in particular, a big, adult male German Shepherd, who was so aggressive that the staff, too frightened to go into him, would throw his food over the top of the door. He could often be heard lunging at the door and sides of his loose box whenever anyone went past. When it was time to feed and clean him, I didn't have the heart to throw his food over the top, knowing some of it would fall on the soiled areas of his kennels, and I worried about him having to live in the mess he made all week. So, when no one was looking,

I decided to go in, broom first so that the broom could take the bites rather than me. I had the bravery that comes with youth and it never occurred to me for a minute that it was possible for a dog to cause me serious harm. He was obviously surprised to see someone, but he moved to the back of the kennel. So I set to work to clean his floor, carefully avoiding eye contact, and moving slowly so I didn't scare him, giving him lots of space to move away when I needed to change places with him.

Once his kennel was clean, I brought in his bowl of food and put it down in the far corner, squatting down away from his food and the door. Being more interested in me than the food, he approached cautiously, sniffing the air around me. He growled when our eyes met, so I dropped mine to prevent him worrying. He came close, sniffing my clothes with all their doggy scents. I talked to him softly, telling him not to worry and raised my arm slowly to touch him. This brought an outburst of growling and he backed off. I learnt not to do that again. Eventually, he came forward for a second time, sniffing my hair and investigating further. Eventually he decided that I was safe and, clearly in desperate need of social contact after spending a week alone, he leant against me. I moved my hand slightly, really slowly this time, to stroke his throat and soon we were great friends.

I hadn't told the other staff that he would allow me to stroke him in case I got into trouble, but I did say it was safe to put his food in through the door, and go in quietly to clean his kennel. One day, just before he went home, he managed to slip past a member of staff and suddenly he was running down the corridor towards me, hackles up, highly aroused and looking scary. At first, I was just another person to be frightened of that was blocking his route home, but then, when he was close enough to smell me, he recognized me and I could sense his immediate relief. I was able to take his collar and walk him back, to the amazement of the staff member who had let him escape and was still standing by his door.

When dealing with Chesil, I knew she wasn't scared, but that she was willing to defend her possession with enough force to do damage, in the same way that the German Shepherd would have protected himself if he had felt threatened by me. Although I found this hard to understand, not being the possessive type myself, I knew it wasn't a good idea to force her into that situation again, so I thought long and hard to find an alternative way to teach her.

A few days later, I was in the kitchen in the early evening before Grant arrived home when I noticed Spider's tennis ball on the side next to the treat bag that we took out with us on walks. Taking a chance, I threw the ball past Chesil who raced after it, pouncing and catching it quickly. I began praising her as soon as she picked it up and some long-remembered game brought her running to me, wagging and growling at the same time. She was in conflict. She wanted to come and show me her ball, proud of what she was doing and happy that I was praising her for being so clever, but she didn't want me to take it. Knowing her ambivalence made her unpredictable, I kept still and kept praising her, and she kept walking, wagging and growling.

I was relaxed as she came towards me for the third time. It was easier for me now that she was free and able to make her own choices and I was not the direct cause of her aggression. I moved the treats closer to the side so she could see them and she dropped her ball in anticipation, coming forward to try to lick the treats off the counter and into her mouth. I quickly moved them out of her reach. The ball was now near my foot so I kicked it, making sure she was looking up so that she wouldn't go for my foot as it moved towards her ball. She saw the ball rocket past her out of the corner of her eye and she turned and sped after it, leaving the treats now that her precious toy was in danger.

When she brought it back this time, I carefully placed my hand down at her nose height before she returned so I would be in a position to catch the ball if she dropped it again. This time, she came forward to sniff the treats but, seeing my hand, she tucked her head in and down so I couldn't take her toy. Now she was in a dilemma. Keep the ball and don't get a treat, or lift her head to get the treat and risk losing the ball. It was her choice. I was hoping she would make the right choice, but it was up to her. I tried to make it more likely by keeping things friendly, praising her and telling her how clever she was. Eventually, she lifted her head, slowly and reluctantly, watching my hand carefully, ready to dodge away at any minute if her precious ball was in danger. High above her head, I turned the treat over in my fingers with the other hand and, suddenly, her mind on the food, she dropped the ball, which fell neatly into my hand waiting below. Yes! Our first retrieve. I was so pleased, and amazed it had been so easy. This was so much better than forcing her to come to me using the line. I immediately rewarded her with a treat and lots of praise and, when she had finished swallowing, I threw the ball again. This time, as she came past me on her lap of honour, excited and pleased from the thrill of doing something clever, I stroked her sides, being careful to keep well away from her head, but sharing in her enjoyment of the moment.

As with all training, just as I thought Chesil had got it, I couldn't get her to repeat it. She either wouldn't approach, preferring to play with the ball by herself, or, if she did come up, she kept her head down and wouldn't let go of the toy. My heart would beat faster as she came rushing towards me growling, eager to get the treat. Up close, my hands were right next to her large teeth and powerful jaws. Having seen them puncture a stolen tin can,

I was fully aware of the damage they could do. And then, just as suddenly, she retrieved perfectly three times in a row. She had got it. She was a smart dog and, given time, she had worked out for herself that it was better to give the ball than to play by herself and that I, for my part of the bargain, would give a treat and give the ball back.

Ecstatic, I showed Grant when he got home and he seemed impressed but not as enthusiastic as me. I was slightly demoralized by his lack of interest as I knew this was a significant breakthrough. Other things overshadowed the training for a few days, and I lacked the motivation to practise. A few days later we were all in the kitchen when Grant said, 'Watch this.' He took a ball from behind the bread bin, threw it for Chesil, she chased it and returned it to him with no trouble. He passed her a treat and turned to grin at me, waiting for my approval. Grant had been secretly practising without me and they could do it seamlessly. His apparent lack of interest was actually an intense focus on the mechanics of the operation. He had been so busy watching what I was doing and trying to remember it that he hadn't had time to be as jubilant as me. I was so pleased, and satisfied that we had found a way that worked for all of us, and really proud of Grant for being successful in what could have been quite a dangerous procedure.

We tried a retrieval game in the garden and it worked there after a few false starts. Then we tried it outside in the fields and it worked there too, soon becoming something that Chesil liked to do above all else. With a ball and a tennis racket, we could finally provide all the safe exercise she so desperately needed and she would return from walks happy and content. The stress lines on her face caused by anxiety about life with us began to disappear and she was like a different dog. Playing with a ball ranked much higher than rolling in dead foxes and chasing sheep. At last, we had something that she wanted that we could use to get her back from even the most desirable of her pastimes and now, with a bit more training, we would have her under control on walks.

In addition to the toy play, Chesil's training to respond to voice cues had begun and was going well. She had learnt the sit cue from an early age and, since the reward was usually food, she would turn to face you and plonk her bottom down as fast as possible, even if she was moving in the other direction when she heard the word.

One evening, I decided to try to teach her the 'down' cue in the kitchen using a food lure. My technique was to keep the treat tight against her nose but also firmly between my fingers until she lay down, as required. Dogs have a very fair sense of possession, so I knew she would never dream of being aggressive over something that I was holding. Once the possession had passed to her, it was a different matter, but as long as I could hold on, there was no danger.

Luring puppies into the down position with food is easy and takes a matter of minutes. Chesil, however, wasn't used to following a lure and wasn't keen on putting herself in a vulnerable position right up close to me. Fortunately, her love of food helped her quickly overcome any reservations and, after several minutes of rewarding good tries, I finally managed to get her to lay down.

As with all Chesil's training, once she had learnt something once, it was like a switch being flipped in her head. Of all the dogs I've trained in my life, she was up there with the very brightest. She didn't know very much to start with, but what she did learn, she learnt very quickly. We progressed rapidly from a lure to a hand-signal, and, after a few days, to just a voice cue. This progress was helped by Spider, who knew hand-signals and voice cues and would throw himself to the ground in hopeful anticipation of a treat. Although dogs don't learn well from copying, having Spider helpfully demonstrating the position gave her time and space to work out what was required without any distractions.

Since learning the down cue was such a positive training experience, it became fun to ask Chesil to do it. She would throw herself down, all four legs collapsing at once, tail wagging, tongue lolling every time. We would give the cue more and more excitedly, hoping for an even faster performance, but being careful not to wear out her enthusiasm.

I hadn't expected Grant's enthusiasm for training, but he was as determined as his dog. Consequently, he drilled Chesil in all things I taught them, over and over when I wasn't there until, when I saw them next, they would have it perfected. I am much more permissive when it comes to training, but only the best performance was good enough for Grant and, with a dog as willing as Chesil, they worked together to get it right.

Although with all the training and ball-playing on walks Chesil didn't have much time for finding smelly messes to roll in, it only took a second for her to catch a scent and track it down, delighting in the act of rolling and the stench afterwards. The smell was very unpleasant for us and we kept a sponge and detergent outside, walking her down to the small stream at the bottom of the road to wash her in cold water before she could come back into the house. The water was from underground and, even in high summer, so cold that it made your feet ache if you stood in it for any length of time. Chesil tolerated it well as we used the sponge to massage the detergent into the worst-affected parts then rinsed her off in the freezing-cold water. She was held still by the lead, but during the slightest break in the proceedings she would shake, a wave of back-and-forth motion starting at her heads and rolling down to her tail, covering us all over in freezing, smelly water. We learnt not to stop until she was completely clean.

Gradually, I noticed that she felt the need to roll less and less. Dogs seem to really enjoy the scent of things we find disgusting, such as rotting fish or fox faeces, and many roll just to get covered in a scent they like. Perhaps they find the smell of our perfumes and the flower-like smells we place in our homes disturbing, and especially the smell of the shampoo we bath them in. I've known many dogs who, fresh from the grooming parlour, cannot wait to roll unmentionable substances into their beautifully trimmed and brushed fur. We washed Chesil only in unperfumed detergent to prevent this.

I noticed that any emotionally traumatic experiences, such as a stressful encounter with another dog, or times when we would get cross and give Chesil the cold shoulder, would send her back into a frenzy of rolling again and I developed a new theory that dogs will roll because they are feeling insecure. It is quite natural for insecure dogs to mark their territory more as smell plays such a big role in their lives. Surrounding themselves with their own scent seems to make them feel better, as we used to see with Chesil when she rolled in her own urine. Thankfully that had now stopped and perhaps covering herself in the scents left by other animals in her environment was a weaker version of the same practice. It is hard for us to empathize with this behaviour exactly as we do not have the same relationship with scent. Whatever was happening inside her head, we were very grateful when, over time, with all the positive improvements that were happening in her life, Chesil felt the need to roll less and less and eventually stopped altogether. No more time-consuming visits to the stream bathing her in the freezing water. Eventually we could walk both dogs home and straight into the house.

Slowly, we started to feel like we were getting somewhere. Gradually, bad times when things went wrong were being replaced by more fun times. It had been a long struggle, but we were beginning to see a light at the end of a long dark tunnel. I found myself stroking Chesil's head and beginning to enjoy the experience rather than focusing on the fact that she might bite me. I could see that inside this difficult, broken creature there was a willing, clever and loyal dog waiting to get out. I began to relax my long-held view that she was a disruptive nuisance, and started to think of her as a project that I could work with. I saw glimpses of a dog, deep inside the damaged outer shell, that I could like and live with after all. Perhaps we would be able to make someone of this dog yet. I began to take photographs.

Chapter 8

New addition

WHEN you first meet someone you want to be with forever, you want to spend as much time with them as possible, finding out about them, building the bond, just being together to the exclusion of everyone else. Grant and I had nine happy months of this before Chesil arrived to shatter the harmony. But if Chesil was like a chisel, gradually chipping away at our time and togetherness, the arrival of Grant's daughter onto the scene was like a sledgehammer.

Holly had been living with her mother and, until recently, with Chesil. She was not doing well at school and was slowly going off the rails, getting into trouble more and more frequently. At 16, she was at a difficult age. She had already experienced the separation of her parents at the age of 12, difficult enough for any young person to cope with, and her father was attentive but distant. Holly had gone into meltdown. This formerly bright A-grade student was now getting low grades and heading for the wrong side of the tracks.

Diane thought Holly would benefit from living with her father for a while. Holly on the other hand was less than impressed about the new arrangements as she knew there would be less freedom and less chance to see her boyfriend. At 16 years of age, however, when your parents are paying the bills, it is their prerogative to choose what is best for you. Consequently, two months after Chesil, Holly arrived with suitcases and an attitude.

To say that I was less than impressed is an understatement. Taking on someone else's dog is bad enough, but at least you can be in control of it. A daughter, and a difficult, unhappy daughter at that, was a different thing altogether. It wasn't that I didn't like Holly, but I found it very difficult to cope with her inevitable intrusion on our comfortable life together. I was angry, upset and furious in turns. My perfect man had been dog-less and virtually childless when I met him, which was perfect for me and my lifestyle. Having lived alone with my dogs for at least 15 years, learning to be with a man full time was enough of a challenge. Now things had changed dramatically and not for the better in my opinion. But how could I argue with Grant's need to nurture his child and bring her back to a state of normality? Logically, I couldn't and I knew it, but emotionally I had a very hard time adjusting to this new development.

New addition

At first, the plan was for Holly to stay with Grant for just a few months, long enough to get her back on track so that she could do well in her exams. I wasn't consulted about the new arrangement as I had been with Chesil. I didn't expect to be as, after all, I wasn't living there and the plan was that, once she had got things turned around, she would go back to live with her mother. Deep down, I strongly suspected that this wasn't going to be the case and that once she moved in, she would be there to stay. Despite my attempt not to let it affect me, I was very resentful of the massive changes Holly's arrival caused to our life together and our relationship.

I had met Holly on several occasions and we had got on well. We both had the maturity to know that Grant loved each of us in a very different way, so there was no need for either of us to be jealous or to feel the need to keep him to ourselves. Grant was big-hearted enough to have enough love for both of us and we knew from the outset that we were not going to be rivals for his affections. We both made a big effort to get on well together and were reasonably successful, although things were never really easy between us as we were too much alike. We struggled to form a friendship from the polite distance at which we kept each other. Even if we had been the best of friends, getting on well with a visiting daughter is totally different to having her suddenly living at the home of your new partner.

I still had my own house, even though I had been spending more and more time with Grant, and so, for a while, I withdrew into my lair where I could be safe from all the madness and I could lick my wounds. I wanted to be away from all the upset that both Holly and Chesil brought to Grant's life as they settled in, and I needed time to come to terms with the dramatic change in our circumstances. Spider could, once again, lie upside down on the sofa without concern. Grant was sensible enough not to panic and to let sleeping dogs lie, although I know it worried him greatly. Slowly I began to return to him. I couldn't stay at home forever. I had a relationship to build, a man to be with and now a new dog and a daughter to assimilate into the household.

So I would go over to the house and be with Grant, helping where I could, and withdrawing when it all got too much. I could see Grant was not having an easy time either. He would also have rather had a quiet life with just the two of us and the dogs, and all the changes that happened when his daughter moved in, together with the very real risk of losing me, were stressful for him too. However, his love for his daughter, and his sense of duty were strong and he never questioned, even for one moment, his decision to take her in.

Interestingly, Holly showed similar behaviour to Chesil when she first arrived, running excitedly up and down the stairs and round the house, delighted, after all, to be with her father who she adored. Over the next few weeks, however, it slowly dawned on her, as it had on Chesil, that life with Grant came at a price and that there were rules to be obeyed and chores to be done. Her freedom to do largely what she liked had now been replaced by partial freedom on condition she behaved in an acceptable way. The principles were the same as for Chesil, and the method of implementation similar, although this time I stayed well clear. I was good with dogs, but had no experience with teenagers. I decided early on that this was Grant's struggle and, while I would support him in his attempts to get control, I wasn't going to take an active part. I was still working on Chesil's behaviour after all.

Chesil and Holly seemed slightly wary of each other, a hangover from the previous days when they lived together, and so they passed like ships in the night, sharing the same house but rarely interacting. Holly seemed to have no empathy with Chesil and either treated her indifferently or over-effusively, causing her to jump up, and then shouting at her to get down. It was not a harmonious relationship but, for now, I tried not to notice, knowing that there were more important issues to be tackled first.

One aspect of Chesil's rehabilitation that was completely ruined by Holly's arrival was her habit of stealing food. We had stopped her searching the house for scraps by making sure there were no leftovers or packets of food lying around and by giving her something else to do in the form of playing with toys. This had worked remarkably well, and once Chesil had found something else to make her feel content, she would lie down and relax rather than hunt for another scrap of food in places previously searched many times that day. Her twice-daily exercise sessions, off lead and running flat out after a toy for half an hour, now gave her sufficient endorphins for her to feel content without this constant foraging, and she had become nicer to live with as a result.

Holly would frequently take more food than she needed and then leave her plate lying around to be discovered by Chesil. She wasn't fussy about where she left plates and cups, so the sitting room and Holly's bedroom became frequent hunting grounds for Chesil. I could see all our good work starting to unravel and Chesil going back to her old habits. Sadly, Chesil would then be told off by Holly and Grant for being naughty, even though I would try to intervene on her behalf and tactfully point out that she was only acting on instincts, leaving it to inference that the food shouldn't have been there in the first place. During the resulting argument between Grant and Holly, as Grant tried to make sure Holly was more careful next time, I would hold my head in my hands and long for a time before the dog and the daughter arrived.

Gradually, Grant's training took effect and Holly became more careful and tidy. It took a while but slowly things improved. Occasional lapses, however, meant that Chesil was periodically rewarded for scavenging in the house, a reward regime well known to firmly cement a learnt behaviour. Holly would, for example, casually leave a huge expensive bunch of grapes in the sitting room, while she wandered off into the kitchen to talk to her dad. Chesil, of course, would waste no time in eating the whole lot. At times like this I despaired and tried to calculate how long it would be before she left home.

On the flip side, it was exciting to have a new daughter to play with. She was entertaining and fun when in the right mood and she brightened our lives with her pink pencil cases and notebooks that seemed to litter every available surface. She wasn't bad or naughty. She didn't take drugs and wasn't surly or uncommunicative as some teenagers can be. I tried to treat her like a little sister and she helped me to remember what it was like to be 16, full of hope for the future and with a carefree attitude that was more about fun than work. On good days, we would go out together as a little family, which was a very novel experience for me after living alone for so long, and I enjoyed it. On bad days, I would leave Grant to sort her out and reconfirm boundaries while I ran home to the sanctuary of my own house.

One area where Holly was great with Chesil was in learning to walk her well on the lead. As she was still in education, she was used to taking instruction and acting on it. Consequently, she mastered the art of walking Chesil on a loose lead very quickly. Chesil had pulled like a train when she first arrived. Determined to get everywhere in the shortest possible time, she would round her shoulders and put her tremendous weight into hauling whoever was unlucky enough to be behind her. In the past, the family had resorted to taking her to a trainer. But he was a bully, used to intimidating easy-going dogs into doing what he wanted. When he kicked her in the face for getting ahead of him, he wasn't prepared for her spirited defence. Her aggressive display left him shocked and humiliated, and he deemed her untrainable. His actual words were 'That bloody dog's mad, it wants putting down.' The family went back to being towed around.

When Chesil came to live with us, I was determined that she would learn to walk nicely on the lead. Although it is far easier to teach a puppy not to pull, there was no reason why Chesil couldn't learn despite her many years of dragging people around after her. Taking the dogs out is one of the ways I relax and unwind and starting a walk with a dog that is throwing itself in one direction and then another with no control is no fun. So from the very first moment, I employed a very simple regime of stopping when the lead was tight and encouraging her to return to my side for a treat, then setting off again when she was relaxed and under control. Spider was very responsive to the recall cue and so he ran free while I concentrated on Chesil's training. This meant I could take him out as well without him being a distraction or getting frustrated by Chesil's lack of progress.

The most difficult part of the process was stopping Chesil's forward movement. Before we slimmed her down, she was large and built like a tank. When she hurled herself forward, it was as much as I could do to stop her. But, after years of dog training, my timing was good and with both hands holding the handle of the lead tight into my waist and by leaning back at the moment of impact, I could almost stop her in her tracks. At first, we didn't progress very rapidly. Four years of towing people behind her had taught her to just keep hauling if humans got sticky; they would move eventually. I had to teach her that this human didn't move at all until she had come back to be beside me. Being the fast learner that she is, Chesil soon discovered that, if I stopped, a treat would become available. We were cutting down her food bit by bit to bring her weight down gradually, so she was very willing to work for treats, but she also wanted to forge ahead so she learned to yo-yo, racing forward, then stopping and running back to get her treat.

It wasn't easy on the outward journey when she was full of energy, but I persevered. Her yo-yoing became less as she lost enthusiasm for the outward run once she discovered she couldn't get any further and there were rewards to be had for staying with me. One day, as we approached the field where I would let her off, she trotted beside me like a dog destined for Crufts and I felt very proud. Then she made a huge unexpected forward lunge for the gate, nearly pulling me off my feet and dragging me around through the edge of a big puddle, splashing us both until we were dripping in muddy water. I realized we still had a way to go before we could walk out easily together.

With Chesil being such a quick learner, it wasn't long before she understood that the less she pulled on the lead, the faster I would walk. Once she had discovered this, she tried hard not to make the lead go tight. I tried hard to give her as much lead as possible, so that it was easier for her to achieve this, and to move at approximately her walking speed. Grant is much stronger than I am and so being pulled was less of a problem for him. Of all the exercises I taught them both, this is the one he was worst at. For him, the idea of stopping just as you've got going, really didn't appeal. He would do it if I asked him but, most of the time, he was content to let her pull. Being a smart dog, Chesil learnt there was one rule for him and another for me and walked perfectly for me whereas she wouldn't for him.

When Holly began to take Chesil out, I showed her the technique of stopping and then rewarding when she was back by her side. Holly got it in an instant and was amazed at how Chesil would now walk by her side instead of out in front. Holly would stop automatically, without being reminded, when the lead began to tighten. With a bit of persistence, for the first time ever, Holly could enjoy taking Chesil for walks without being towed, and I was proud of them both.

It was while walking with Chesil at heel one day that I discovered that being careless with food delivery can have unexpected consequences. While Spider ran ahead carrying his ball on a walk, I was practising Chesil's heelwork. She was walking nicely, tail waving, waiting expectantly for the treat. As I took the treat out of my pocket, my finger got caught up and instead of the treat falling straight into her open mouth as usual, it bounced off my coat and down the front of my leg. Quick as a flash, Chesil was on it, biting down on it hard to prevent it falling to the floor. She has strong jaws, as do all dogs that have a round heads with plenty of room for the muscles that close the mouth. Spider's head is long and narrower, giving him a comparatively weaker bite than the wider-jawed, shorter faced Chesapeake. Due to her earlier operation for jaw cancer that had removed one of her lower canines, Chesil overcompensated for her lost tooth and brought her upper jaw down hard to save the treat from falling. My leg, as well as the treat, was in the way and I felt a sharp stabbing pain as her upper canine sunk into me. She hadn't meant to do it but she tore a small hole in my jeans and left me with a wound that gave me a small scar. Later, I would often point to either the hole in my old jeans that I still wore or the scar, teasing Grant by saying 'Look, that's where Chesil bit me!' For now, I yelled loudly as the pain hit and she shot sideways, shocked by my reaction. After that, she was a little more careful at catching the treats and I know I was more careful with delivery.

Chapter 9

Mr Policeman

SPIDER loved to carry a toy in his mouth, rushing to get it when he got excited and greeting us tail wagging, mouth full of fluffy rabbit. He looked so lovely when he did this, his coat shining, his body soft and flowing, with the fluffy rabbit dangling from either side of his face, and it made him seem less daunting to people who were not used to being greeted by an enormous black dog. As Spider paraded close to them, visitors would often misinterpret his intentions, thinking he had brought them a present. They would try to take it, only to find he would cleverly evade them, turning his head at the last moment so their hand closed on thin air. He hadn't brought it to them, he just liked carrying it and, in the excitement of the moment, wanted to play his favourite game. I kept his toy box beside my front door and he would stand next to it ready to snatch up a toy as soon as he heard me starting to welcome someone inside.

To make sure Spider felt at home in Grant's house, I had taken over a multi-coloured soft toy that he loved and he often carried it around when he felt happy, rushing to the door to greet Grant with it in his mouth when he came home. Grant, who was now developing a happy, easy-going relationship with Spider, would regularly bring it in for him from the garden after we had left, and, when we arrived at his house, it would be waiting for him on the shoe rack by the front door. As we entered the house, Spider would snatch it up in his jaws without breaking his stride as he raced in to find out where Grant was. Chesil seemed to know that this was Spider's toy and didn't touch it.

One day in the garden when we were all sitting outside enjoying the sun, Chesil was feeling particularly playful and began bouncing around the garden looking for something to do. Spotting Spider's toy, she began to play with it, tossing it up into the air, trying to catch it, then pouncing on it and shaking it as if to kill it when it landed on the ground near to her. It was clear that she had played this game many times when left alone as a puppy. It was a harmless game and Spider was happy to share his toy so we watched Chesil having fun, happy to see her settled enough at last to want to initiate play.

As her energy began to run low, she lay down with the toy, nuzzling and poking it with her nose. Then she began to chew. Bits of the stuffing started to appear and

I could see that if I didn't stop her, Spider's toy would soon be torn to pieces. Walking round behind her, I took her collar and pulled upwards. Taken by surprise, she exploded into aggression, growling and snarling, but grabbing the toy before she was pulled away from it. 'Drop it,' I commanded in a loud, strong voice, more for the benefit of Grant than Chesil. I knew she had no idea what I meant, but I thought I'd say it anyway since I was now standing on the lawn holding a spitting, grumpy dog up in the air with front feet slightly off the ground, her mouth fortunately too full of toy to whip round and bite me.

If I stood there long enough, I knew she would have to drop it and I could reclaim the toy. She was heavy and I wondered how long I could keep it up, but I couldn't stop now I had started or I would lose the edge I had carefully created over the past months. Seeing my predicament, Grant hurried over to help. Realizing there was little he could do, he tried shouting at her to 'Leave it.' It had worked in the past. This time, Chesil wasn't going to be intimidated and held on.

As we all stood there, wondering what would happen next, a large, black dog-shaped object exploded into our field of vision. Unexpectedly and seemingly from nowhere, Spider launched himself at Chesil's face, delivering a mighty, explosive roar and presenting all his teeth for her inspection. She dropped the toy immediately, I let go of her collar and she scuttled off, leaving a satisfied Spider and the toy on the floor.

We were amazed. Spider is a placid dog and doesn't like to get into trouble. He had the occasional fight with other dogs when he was young, but only in self-defence. He was bigger than most dogs so he would usually use his chest to flatten them if they started anything, growling loudly while he held them in place. Unlike Chesil, who seemed to love a good scrap, he would hang back and weigh things up, getting involved only if there was no other choice. So for him to take on Chesil when she hadn't done anything directly to him was surprising. His reasons were unknown, although I strongly suspect that he had watched her behaviour, noticed that Grant had been unable to sort it out and, worrying that we were at risk, had waded in with his own successful brand of action to finish it off once and for all.

Whatever the reason, he was efficient and effective and had solved the problem with minimum energy loss and risk to all persons. I've always marvelled at the way well-adjusted dogs solve issues with just enough force to get the desired result, without leaving other members of the pack frightened of them long term. Chesil bore Spider no ill-will after this incident and wasn't afraid to be near him. Spider had obviously turned up the heat for a reason; she seemed to understand why it was necessary and now it was all over.

Chesil continued to play with Spider's toy after that on occasions. I could see Spider watching her closely as if slightly worried, but he left her in peace. Then, one day, I was making dinner in the kitchen and Chesil was under the table, waiting to dart out like a shark for any food that might just drop off the surfaces as I cooked. During a break in proceedings, Spider came in with his toy and lay down. This was unusual behaviour as he disliked the clanging of pots and pans and usually preferred to lay just outside the kitchen where he could keep me in view but not be so exposed to the noise. He carefully placed his toy down beside his paws, right next to where Chesil was sitting. Again, this was unusual as he would usually put the toy between his paws or casually discard it. This time, the careful placement, just to one side, looked more deliberate.

Chesil was sitting under the table, the top of her head close to the underside so I couldn't see her eyes. I saw her move forward slightly as if to take the toy. Spider looked up at her, then down at his toy, then back at her. I knew there would be a fight if she tried to snatch it. Perhaps she did too. She sat back slightly. Spider waited. The toy was equidistant between them. She stood up, her head now slightly closer to the toy, and she looked at it longingly. Spider waited. Then, suddenly, she turned and went back into the depths of the table, leaving all thoughts of the toy behind. Spider grabbed the toy and tossed it in the air, then got up and walked out to lie in his usual place, on the soft carpet in the hall with his head protruding into the kitchen so he could see what was going on.

After that, they shared the toy. Chesil didn't have much interest in it, but Spider didn't worry about it when she played with it. If someone was coming home and the toy was right next to Chesil, Spider would go and grab it without a second thought as if it was now his right to do so and he no longer worried that she would guard it.

It was not always this harmonious, though. Spider and Chesil had several fights in the early days. These were mostly in the sitting room when Chesil, seeing that Spider was getting lots of fuss from me, would try to rudely barge in on the action. Chesil didn't do anything subtly and, seeing that affection was now on offer, she would launch herself at me, abruptly halting our quiet cuddling session and disrupting the peace.

After several such launches, Spider decided enough was enough. Next time, without warning, he exploded into aggression as Chesil approached, snarling and showing his teeth. Spider is bigger than Chesil, but that wasn't going to prevent her from fighting back. So, in the middle of the sitting room, with Grant and I plastered against the sofas out of the way, they had a huge fight.

Now I have witnessed enough dog fights to know that it's not a good idea to get involved. I had seen the awful injuries on the hands and arms of rescue staff and owners after they had done so. Fighting dogs are highly aroused and thinking only of victory or self-defence. Usually, however, unless one of the dogs has very limited experience with other dogs, they are fighting by the unwritten canine rules of engagement, which means that there is a lot of noise but no injury. Although it may sound like they are killing each other, they will quickly stop and there won't be a scratch on either of them, apart from small tooth marks that were caused by accident. If humans interfere, all thoughts of a fair fight get put aside and the fighting moves into survival mode. There is now a risk that any or all of the parties will get badly bitten. I also knew these dogs' characters well and, given how long they had been together, I suspected there was little likelihood of lasting damage. Some superficial accidental wounds, perhaps, but nothing serious.

I knew this, but Grant didn't. To him, it looked like his precious blond Chesapeake was the victim of an unwarranted and unnecessary assault and his instinct was to help her. I had to stop him getting involved. 'Just leave them,' I said, calmly and confidently, hoping they would soon stop. I could see him poised to intervene. The sight of the dog he loved upside down beneath a gigantic black snarling beast was nearly more than he could bear. He is a man of action and not used to watching from the sidelines. I knew that if he intervened now, just as Spider was finishing giving Chesil this lesson, he would have to repeat it later, so I summoned all the superiority that being an expert in this field could give me and ordered him to leave them to it.

Very quickly in real time, although it seemed like a lifetime to us, they broke apart and we examined our respective dogs for wounds. Following this, and the numerous fights, that followed, a few little nicks and scratches were all that was left and Grant began to relax a little more when they started. None of us enjoyed witnessing these fights and we tried to prevent them if we could but, just as we were teaching Chesil lessons she didn't enjoy, so was Spider. He had a louder, more aggressive way of doing it, but it was relatively short-lived and effective. He always gave Chesil the chance to stop what she was doing before he followed it up by clearly signalling to her with body language, but if she deliberately ignored him, he would take action. After quite a short time, Chesil came to respect Spider so that a look or a posture was enough to stop her doing something he didn't like. This was really useful for us since the rules that he was imposing, such as not to be such a nuisance at mealtimes, or not to pester visitors, were also those that we were trying to teach.

Mr Policeman

We started to call Spider 'Mr Policeman Dog' as he began to patrol whenever we ate our dinner on our laps in front of the TV. Chesil was a real nuisance over food in the early days and would either edge slowly closer, trying to get near enough to lick the side of the plate, or she would launch herself towards the food, forcing us to take evasive action. Spider had never had the opportunity to steal food from plates during his puppyhood so he didn't do this, and he provided an obvious contrast to Chesil who had learnt some really bad habits in her previous life. She was really sneaky about it, too, having learnt not to make a direct approach but to sidle up and wait until we weren't paying attention. I once saw her sit next to a visitor, push her nose into his hand for some fuss and then slide her tongue into his tea when he wasn't looking! Spider watched our feeble attempts to keep Chesil at bay and to gently tell her 'no' and eventually decided to help us out. Now that she had more respect for him, all he had to do was walk up and down between us and her, staring at her if she got too close, and she would back off. He was really useful and, eventually, taught her not to do this, making his patrols unnecessary.

As time went on, Spider's need to use violence became less as she became more respectful and, eventually, he just had to stare in her direction to make her stop what she was doing. The last time I remember him using force was one day when I was sitting eating something on the sofa before Grant came home from work. Chesil had edged closer to me and was trying to move her head far enough forward to sneak a quick lick. I had asked her to go away and pushed her back a few times, but she persisted. I could then feel Spider pressing against my leg from the other side as he attempted to manoeuvre her backward. He was staring forcefully, but she wasn't taking any notice, her eyes fixed on my food. Suddenly, he growled and grabbed the skin at the top of her head in his mouth. She kept still, resolute about wanting the food, eyes facing the plate. I could see him squeezing harder, she winced but didn't back off. He squeezed harder still and, this time, she had to concede defeat. She moved away. After that, I never saw her deliberately 'disobey' him again.

In the early days, I didn't trust Chesil not to bite me unexpectedly. All my years of practice with unpredictable dogs had taught me enough to keep myself safe and avoid obvious situations that may provoke her into getting upset. Sooner or later, however, I would need to get closer to her and begin to teach her to trust that I wouldn't hurt her when I handled her. Due to some botched treatment for ear problems earlier in her life, she would always turn to bite someone who touched her ears. Although she never actually made contact with the skin, it was still frightening when she turned on you if your hands absentmindedly strayed to her ears, and the experience would leave your heart racing and your nerves jangling. She wasn't overly impressed with being manhandled either if you wanted to check her for ticks or otherwise give her the once-over. Having never learnt to feel comfortable about being handled, I knew that she had a long way to go in this area.

It takes a long time to earn that trust on both sides when you take on a dog, especially if it has a previous history of aggression to humans. So I worried about her, she worried about me and we skirted around each other, coming into contact regularly but not pushing our boundaries too far too soon.

With Grant it was different. He has no fear of being bitten and expects dogs not to do so. He would handle Chesil with confidence and assurance, rolling her unceremoniously onto her back to check her tummy for ticks that the dogs so often collected from the sheep fields. Only I noticed her stiffness and her concern. She wasn't aggressive towards him, but I could tell she wasn't relaxed either. So I tried to introduce regular handling sessions, in a gradual, non-threatening way, a bit at a time so she developed a tolerance to it. In the early days, I would do so reluctantly, often feeling the prickles of fear up my arm as I realized I had gone a bit too far and my hand was now in danger of being bitten. I was determined to undo the damage that had previously been done by rough handling of her ears and we developed a game of 'ears up, ears down' where I would lift her ears gently and then bring them down, followed by lots of fuss and praise.

Gradually, we both began to relax, and I started to get down on the floor beside her where she would feel more comfortable with me being on her level, rather than choosing to touch her from the relative safety of the sofa. During these sessions, she would seize the opportunity to get close, pushing herself relentlessly against me as I struggled not to overbalance and be pushed over. Sometimes these sessions would become too much for both of us. I would become concerned that her intentions were more about wanting to push me around and flatten me rather than just wanting cuddles, and she would become frantically excited, bashing against me, hurting me and digging her nails in. At these moments, Mr Policeman Spidy would intervene, slowly weaving his way between us, edging her out and keeping me safe. This could have been a very clumsy way of playing, but I still feared it would end in an aggressive outburst if I found myself underneath her heavy body. When I learnt Spider would protect me, I took more risks with Chesil, getting her used to being handled in a much shorter time than I would have done without his help. If he was there, I felt safe. Slowly she learnt that I meant no harm, that I wouldn't hurt her when I pulled her legs or touched her ears or belly, and she began to relax. Her excited outbursts became less and Spider relaxed his patrols, although he always watched over me, just in case.

One of Chesil's oddities was the way she greeted people. She would run up to them, excited to see them, particularly if it were Holly or Grant, and try to get as close to their face as possible. Nothing unusual in that but, once she got there, she would go completely still. As someone who has spent a lot of time around dangerous dogs, I know that this stillness usually precedes an aggressive outburst and so I found it very unnerving. It is also unusual. Sociable dogs usually wriggle and squirm, happy to be back with their friends. Chesil's frozen, wide-eyed expression was not normal.

Interestingly, Holly had a similar way of greeting people. She would run up, smiling widely but slightly falsely, very still, watching the person intently with her big eyes, waiting for signs of acceptance. I realized that both Chesil and Holly were uncertain of how they would be received. Being brushed aside when you want approval is difficult for any young social animal and is a powerful punishment, even if it is an unintentional one.

In addition to sometimes being friendly, and sometimes only having time for a quick hello, Grant did not like being licked by dogs, considering it something that is both mucky and unappealing. Having never lived at close quarters with a happy pet dog when younger, he hadn't learnt to accept this as part of what dogs do. Spider quickly found out, from Grant's explosions of disapproval when he did it, that it was unacceptable to lick him in greeting. Spider continued to lick my face when saying hello as he had always done, but he would just plant his whiskery face as close to Grant's as he dared and be content to be near him.

Chesil, however, from puppyhood, had never been quite sure of her reception when racing to greet the much-loved members of her family. Sometimes they would be happy to see her, and sometimes she would be rejected as they were too busy with other things. Sometimes they were cross with her when she jumped on them, and other times they would hug her. Knowing how difficult they were to please, she would have tried to pacify them by licking their faces. When this was met with vigorous disapproval, she must have lost all confidence about the way she would be received.

Once I realized this, I tried to give both Chesil and Holly undivided attention and approval during greetings. This wasn't difficult for me as I would be pleased to see them both, especially after a long day alone working at my computer. Grant also began to change his way of greeting them once I had made him aware of what the problem was, making it a priority to say hello straight away to all those awaiting his affection. I tried to let Chesil know that it was safe to greet in a more exuberant way, but habits taught in puppyhood are often set in stone, and it was a long time before she became more relaxed when saying hello. Eventually, however, both Holly and Chesil lost some of their stiffness on greeting and, now, more assured of their reception, they began to settle down and enjoy the process of saying hello when reuniting with members of the household.

While it was easy to diagnose and treat small idiosyncrasies like the way Holly and Chesil greeted people, I knew that they both had other behavioural issues that ran deeper and needed more fixing. I just didn't have the knowledge or qualifications for helping with Holly and so had to leave it all to Grant, staying out of the way or giving support where I could.

One of Holly's less-than-attractive traits at that time was talking non-stop at you if she got the chance, hardly pausing for breath, about anything and everything that came into her head, never once giving you a chance, or wanting you to say anything in return. Although I realized this came from a lack of self-esteem, it was very trying, especially since I have a much more reserved and empathetic approach to conversation, waiting thoughtfully while the other person finishes what they are saying before I respond. Holly missed my subtle signals altogether, being so wrapped up in her own world, so I did my best to nod in the right places, give her the reassurance that she needed, and then stay out of her way so that she couldn't catch me again next time. I hoped that, in time, she would grow out of it. Until then, the relationship between Grant and I sat on a knife-edge, with neither of us really knowing if I could hang on long enough to ride this particularly heavy-duty storm that life had thrown at us so soon after we had first met.

Chapter 10

Serious solutions

I'D JUST arrived at Grant's house and was putting my bag and keys down in the kitchen when I saw a strange sight through the window. Grant and Holly were hunched over a wriggling Chesapeake in the garden. It looked as though they were trying to pin her down, a very risky procedure with Chesil and, I thought, unusually brave for them. She was resisting but not aggressively, and they were taking it in turns to order her to 'Keep still, Chesil!' Neighbours observing the spectacle would have wondered what form of strange torture we had cooked up for her now.

Going out into the garden, I could see that Holly had a bag of treats and was shovelling them into Chesil's mouth to keep her occupied, while Grant was clipping her nails as fast as he dared. They were both partially leaning on her to keep her from getting up and, when Holly ran out of the treats she held in her hand, there was furious wriggling from Chesil in her attempts to get free while Holly got more from the bag.

'Keep feeding her, Holly,' Grant yelled as he struggled to keep hold of Chesil's paw and clip another nail before she bit him. Her face was turned towards his hand and her nose was wrinkled into a snarl.

'I am!' protested Holly as she distracted Chesil away from his hand and the clippers with the next mound of treats.

Finally it was all over. Chesil was released and she sprang up, shaking herself as if to remove the indignity of it all. Grant and Holly looked exhausted, frazzled and relieved that it was all over.

Cutting Spider's nails was a very different affair. He would lie on the sofa while I gently cut the tips off his huge claws. He has black nails and, although I have had lots of experience with cutting dog's nails, I was wary of clipping too much and cutting the quick with all its nerves and blood vessels, so I did it often and just took a little bit off at a time. Many owners prefer to take their dogs to vets or other professionals for nail-clipping but, depending on who does it, it can be a frightening and unnerving experience for dogs to be manhandled in such a way by strangers. For this reason, I preferred to do it myself. No fuss, no drama. I'd been doing it all his life and it held no fear for Spider – he lay still, quiet and relaxed. We had to find a better solution for Chesil.

The best way would have been to gradually desensitize her to having her paws held, then to the feel of the clippers pressed against them, and finally the pressure of the painless cutting action, all made easier with the generous use of treats to change the emotion from fear to pleasure. All very well in theory but time raced by and I noticed, one day, that her nails were now long again and we hadn't done any work with her. She was standing on the step after being dried from a swim in the river when I noticed, so, taking a chance, I ran to get the necessary equipment. Returning with a bag of treats and the clippers, I asked her to sit. I slowly lifted a paw and moved the clippers towards it, the bag of treats lying temptingly on the step beside her. As the clippers moved towards the nail, her whole face wrinkled, spectacularly exposing her front teeth.

It's a good sign when dogs are prepared to warn you first before they bite. It gives you time to consider your actions and whether you really want to continue. Some people punish growls and snarls, fearing that this is an aggressive act and perhaps embarrassed that their dog is being difficult. What these people don't realize is that this is just a precursor of a much more aggressive act and real violence is to follow if they don't stop what they are doing. If you get rid of this early warning system by punishing a dog, it has no way to communicate it is unhappy, worried or fearful. After all, dogs cannot speak to us and tell us, so watching and acting on signals that all is not well, even if they are alarming, keeps you safe and gives the dog a chance to save real aggression for when it's really needed.

Chesil was telling me, very obviously, that she wasn't happy. I acknowledged this but I wanted to proceed and get the job done. She wasn't growling, and it had been a slow wrinkling of the nose so I wasn't in too much danger right now. I dropped her paw and gave her a treat. Some people would say that this was rewarding her 'bad' behaviour. I would say that I had seen that she was unhappy and said 'okay, I understand, then I won't go any further' and, to show my good intentions, given her a treat. I've found, in the past, that most dogs respond well when someone listens to them, relieved to have found, at last, a human that understands what they are trying to say.

I tried again. This time I got the clippers to the nail before there was a slight wrinkling of the nose. Chesil was looking intently at the bag of treats. I dropped her paw and gave her a treat. I decided to go for a clip the next time so I raised her paw again, brought the clippers close and clipped the long white piece off way below the pink of the quick so I knew there would be no pain. She shifted her weight and brought her head down, face now covered in wrinkles and her exposed teeth close to my hand. I felt the prickling in my hands that told me they were in danger and my heart beat faster. I dropped her paw and gave her a treat. Chesil was now excited and dancing about, relieved to have survived what must have seemed like an attack on her person. I felt the same way. I wanted to try again, but this time decided that I would go for a back paw, being just that little bit further away from those teeth.

The rest of the procedure was uneventful thanks to Chesil quickly realizing that this was a much better way of doing things. The wrinkling of her nose gradually reduced as she learnt that all she had to do was wait for the 'snip' and then a treat would be delivered. She went back to staring intently at the bag of treats while I clipped, as if willing them to come out by themselves, or, perhaps, wanting to think only about the treats rather than what I was doing, and I was able to do all her nails with relative ease. After this breakthrough, I showed Grant and Holly the technique and, although they were both a bit worried about it at first, they settled into a routine that both they and Chesil could cope with. No more wrestling her to the ground and shovelling in treats while her nails were cut. This was a much kinder way for all concerned and better for Chesil's waistline.

Although we were making progress on things like this, there were still odd incidents where Chesil would go back to her previous form. One day in late spring a bag of rubbish had been left in the narrow passageway by the back gate en route to the bin in the front garden. At first,

Grant couldn't understand why she was sitting out there, in a place where she walked through every day but never sat. Going over to investigate, he was met by an angry Chesil, hunched up against the bag, head lowered, pupils wide, teeth on full display and a blood-curdling growl rumbling in her chest.

Chesil hadn't opened the bag of rubbish, so there was no urgency as there would have been if she had been eating the remains of a cooked chicken. So, not wanting to get into a fight, Grant left her and came to tell me. I came out to see for myself and got the same reaction. I moved forward, she hunched and growled, I moved back, she stopped. I danced forward and back for a while, causing her to growl in a rhythm. Grant and I laughed but both knew it wasn't really so funny. I went inside to get the can of compressed air we kept for emergencies such as this, since we couldn't leave her where she was. There was a danger that she might tear open the bag and get sick from eating the contents, or that Holly would come home, get too close and get bitten before we had a chance to warn her.

Cans of compressed air are sold as a dog-training aid, but, in my opinion, are far too severe for normal training. I had been given the can to trial as a behaviourist, and, I knew from the explosively loud whooshing noise it made, that it would be really effective at scaring dogs. So we kept it in case we were ever in a situation with

Chesil that required urgent intervention. This time we wanted to teach her that if we wanted to move through the passageway to get to the gate, we could, whether she wanted to guard a bin bag full of rubbish or not. I gave it to Grant, not wishing to get involved with punishing her. I heard him go out, and then the sharp rush of air from the can and, seconds later, Chesil came in, tail low, defeated. The rubbish went straight to the bin after that.

After that incident, we began to work with empty food packets, clearing them completely of food and then using them like toys to be thrown and retrieved. At first she would grab them, stiffen and rush under the table, expecting to be shouted at. We would praise her and tell her how clever she was to relax her. Her body would soften, then she would come out, looking unconvinced that we meant it, head down so we couldn't snatch the packet back unexpectedly. We invited her to come towards us, and she did so, growling softly to let us know that she would defend her prize if this was a trick to get the packet back. We ignored this and praised her for coming, patting her back and sides when we thought it was safe to do so, but keeping well away from her head. To get the packet back, we would rattle the treat pot, getting her attention with a treat until the packet fell out of her mouth, discarded in favour of the real thing. With a bit of luring one of us would be able to manoeuvre her away, while the other safely picked up the packet off the floor.

Eventually her confidence grew until, one day, she came running to us, head up to return the packet to get her treat. After that we practised with all sorts of low-value food-related items, such as a bone she had lost interest in chewing or a yogurt pot that had been licked clean. Once she could do this easily, we upped our game, asking for higher-value objects, such as a pot that still had traces of yogurt inside.

We were always fair, giving the treat, then giving the pot or packet back. One day I went too far, asking for a chew I had just given her. She did come over, but with her head down growling. I waited and, eventually, she softened and lifted her head to give me the chew. I took it, fed the treat, and then gave her back the chew she had brought plus another from the packet. This two for one policy was a hit and she was never reluctant about giving up chews again.

Food, which had once been Chesil's main pleasure in life and had been so important to her, was beginning to take on less significance now that she was getting plenty of exercise and play. As a result of this, and of our policy of encouraging her to take any food items such as bones to her bed or under the table to eat and then leaving her alone, she began to calm down about eating special items when there were people present. There was a time when you couldn't go into the kitchen if she was eating without her leaving her bone and making a frightening, threatening, growling run at you, sending you scurrying out again, unless you were feeling very brave. Now she would happily chew at her bone on her bed while we were cooking, safe in the knowledge that she would be left alone to eat in peace.

If dogs can be rehabilitated in a few months and big improvements seen, not so daughters. When she first arrived, Holly lashed out frequently at the world around her, and particularly at Grant, as she fought for some control over the events in her life. She was uncertain of her place in the world and low in self-esteem. Sometimes Grant and Holly would have a massive argument as she raged against the new rules or something she considered unfair. Similar in character, both would be shouting and not prepared to back down. This would make Spider shake even if we went to another room, and so I quickly learnt to take both dogs out walking over the fields until it was safe to go back in.

By late summer, following five months under Grant's imposed boundaries and codes of conduct, Holly was beginning to settle down and feel secure. She found a summer job in a local restaurant and had begun the slow process of rebuilding her self-esteem. She had also found a new boyfriend, who we both liked, and things seemed to be going well.

Then, just as things were beginning to look good and the new school term approached, circumstance dictated that her mother, recently remarried, move permanently to France. Holly meanwhile stayed with Grant to do her A Levels at a local college. Even though Holly knew this was the only practical option, she was nevertheless pretty upset and we could all feel Holly's pain.

While we tried to ease it and make things better, I decided not to leave Spider alone in Grant's house when Holly was going to be there alone. He is a sensitive creature and I was concerned that her angst would be transmitted to him and leave him worrying. Having seen how she behaved with Chesil, in an indifferent and sometimes unpleasant way, I just didn't want to leave him alone with her. He had only known kindness from humans and the last thing I wanted was for him to find out that not everyone liked to have him around. So I took to driving him all the way back to my house if we wanted to go out for any length of time. One Sunday we had decided to have a day out fossiling, a favourite pastime of Grant's, near to Chesil beach from which Chesil had got her name. The long journey in the car, followed by much hanging about on rocky shorelines, meant that it was an unsuitable outing for dogs so we left them at home. I had driven Spider to my house where he could get out into the garden via his dog flap if he wanted. Chesil was at home with Holly.

In the afternoon, a hysterical Holly was on the phone. 'I can't do my essays in time,' she sobbed.

'Why aren't you at work?' Grant said, unsympathetically.

Holly worked part-time as a waitress in a local restaurant and was booked to be there in the afternoon. It eventually became apparent that Holly had not done a stack of vital essays for her A-level course work and was now up against the Monday deadline. With the benefit of hindsight, we may have seen that Holly was not coping well and that there were big issues at the new college she was now attending to do her A levels. We may also have realized that some of her panic was due to her being left on her own while we went out without her.

Holly rang several more times, anxious for reassurance but aggravating Grant a little more each time. She sounded increasingly upset and distressed when she called. Eventually, on our return journey, Holly rang again, a little more hysterical and brittle this time.

'Chesil's being naughty,' she said.

'What's she doing?' Grant asked.

'She's guarding a toy in the hall and won't let me past.'

Chesil hadn't done anything like this for a long time so it was a surprise to hear this. 'She's taken one of my teddies out of the bag in the dining room and she's just laying there growling,' Holly said. We were quite close to home so Holly was instructed to stay put, holed up in the living room with her school books.

The bin bag full of Holly's childhood toys had been in the dining room for months while Grant found a suitable place to store them. On the odd occasion Chesil had gone into the dining room, she'd walked straight past the bag of toys, disinterested once she realized they weren't food. So why would she suddenly start playing with the toys now? Was she responding to Holly's distress and looking for something to comfort herself with? Had she deliberately found something that she could use to help her take charge of the situation when she saw Holly was out of control? She could have taken the bear to her favourite hiding place under the kitchen table but had, instead, chosen the place where people had to walk to get to different parts of the house. Or had she just been bored and, looking for something to do, found the bear and taken it to the nearest open space to play with? I had lots of theories, but only Chesil knew for sure.

When we got home, Chesil was still guarding the teddy in the hall. I heard Grant go in and tell her to leave it. Much growling and shouting followed and then Grant came back into the kitchen without the teddy. I was ready with the can of compressed air, too tired and emotionally drained from the dramas of the day to try a food exchange. He went back in and, a moment later, came out victorious. Chesil went back under the kitchen table, tail down, defeated, and Holly, liberated from her prison, ran upstairs to go to the bathroom, and then to the sanctuary of her bedroom. It had been another day of chaos in Grant's house, even thought we weren't there to witness most of it, and I was really glad I had left Spider in the peace and quiet of my own home where he could relax and feel safe.

Chapter 11

Outdoor encounters

'GO ON, go in,' Grant encouraged, urging Chesil into the murky water. We were on the banks of a narrow river with gently sloping sides, which was perfect for teaching a dog to swim. The river ran alongside a footpath through the water meadows where we often walked. Surprisingly, given how lovely it was there, we encountered very few people. However, some horses lived there so we had to be careful to check they were somewhere in the distance before letting Chesil free, in case she decided to chase them. 'Swim! Swim!' Grant urged now that he could see her poised with her feet in the water, excited, ready to wade in. Fearing the unknown, she hesitated, unsure about the dark swirling mass of water, her wagging tail slowing as she concentrated. Then she turned and went back to paddling in the shallows, splashing through the water, tail waving.

I wasn't sure about this method of teaching a dog to swim. I knew it wouldn't have worked for Spider, with his sensitivities and strong desire to keep himself safe. When he was two years old, Spider had still been standing in the shallow water, reaching out as far as he dared to get a ball thrown into deeper water, but no amount of urging could persuade him to go deeper. So one day, while I had a friend staying from Australia – someone to hold my clothes and call the emergency services if I got stuck in the mud – I took off my shoes and jeans and waded into our local shallow lake.

I took Spider's tennis ball with me and, trying to ignore the slime at the bottom that was oozing up through my toes, I threw it into the water in front of me so he had to paddle round my legs to get it. As we got deeper, his paws occasionally left the bottom. In no time at all, and after swimming with him to the other side of the lake and back again, he could swim. He didn't like it much, except on hot days when the cool water felt good on his skin. At these times he would happily swim with big powerful strokes right into the middle of the lake to retrieve his ball. He could swim efficiently and for a long time without the panicky, splashing, exhausting motion that dogs use when they first start, their paws coming up too high as they worry about keeping their head out of the water. I was pleased that I had taken things slowly so that Spider had no fear of deep water now.

Chesil was a different kind of dog, though. She didn't worry too much about her personal safety and was always up for anything. She could be stirred up easily, and, once aroused, would attempt anything she thought might be fun. Swimming turned out to be one of these things she wanted to try.

Chesapeakes have the genes for swimming. Their bodies are covered in a woolly coat and they secrete more oil from their skin glands than other breeds, giving them a distinctive smell and causing their ears to need regular cleaning. This oily coat protects them from the cold and they are relatively insensitive to sensation, so even very cold water has little effect on them. They also have the brave temperament that allows them not to worry about how far away from the shore they are swimming or what may be lurking beneath the surface – their focus is simply on bringing home that fallen goose, or, in our case, the thrown tennis ball. Swimming is great exercise for dogs, especially if you live near rivers with cool, fresh water like we did. It cleans them and cools them in the summer and can be a source of great fun for them, too. We knew Chesil would love it if we could just get her to try it.

We didn't use a ball to encourage Chesil to swim at first. It was still early in the year and the water was cold. Spider didn't like swimming when it was cold and I wasn't going to make him swim to retrieve a ball I had thrown for Chesil, but that she probably wouldn't fetch. So Grant tried the encouragement method instead. At first, it was not successful. Further along the riverbank there was another place to try. Grant has a very persistent temperament, just like his dog, and, while I am more easy-going preferring to let dogs do their own thing and would have let it go, he kept on trying. Still no success, but this time she went in further and, being a shallower place, she was able to bound up and down the river, searching out new scents and having great fun in the water. When we returned to our original place, with a little bit of urging from Grant, she was in first time.

On her first go, she surprised herself, her head going deeper than she intended, her heavy body causing her to sink suddenly, making her try to rear up to shake her ears free of the water. This caused her to thrash wildly with her front legs, trying to get enough height to get her head out of the water. Soon, however, she settled down into a rhythm and you could see she was a natural. She revelled in the experience. Whereas Spider would always rush in, swim for the ball and then turn for home, Chesil swam like an otter, just for the love of doing it, back and forth, investigating under the bridge, pushing against the current and then enjoying the speed and thrill as she turned to swim with it, her strong legs powering her through the water as if she had been doing it all her life.

Once she had discovered the delights of swimming, there was no turning back. We took her to the swimming hole as often as possible and she would race ahead of us to get into the water. Once she had learnt to retrieve a ball, we would throw the ball for her again and again until she hardly had the strength to heave herself up the bank. She learnt to throw herself into the water from the bank to save scrambling down. Spider wasn't so keen on swimming and wanted to run, so we threw the ball across the stream for him, he would run through the shallow part, chase the ball down on the field the other side, bring it back and wait on the far bank. We would ask him to 'drop', and he would drop the ball with a satisfying plop into the river. Chesil would launch herself from the bank, usually land on top of the ball and then turn circles in the water trying to locate it. She would return it to us and we would start the game all over again.

Taking the dogs to the swimming hole became a routine for us after work as the evenings drew out. It became a way of keeping Chesil's strong Chesapeake odour, caused by the excess oil in her coat and ears, at bay. It was also a great way to exercise her and we would come home with dogs that slept quietly and contentedly all evening.

One evening, when I was away working, Grant went down to the river with Chesil by himself. Instead of taking the ball, he took a toy pheasant into which we had sewn some balls so that it would float. As he was returning home in his country clothes, Chesil on the lead and proudly carrying her bedraggled pheasant, head and tail held high, a driver passing them on the road wound his window down and angrily exclaimed, 'I suppose you've just shot that!' Grant was temporarily speechless, Chesil pulled towards the car and wagged her tail. Grant, amused now that he had recovered himself, allowed Chesil to move forward to show her trophy and prove their innocence, saying, 'We can try resurrecting it if you like.' Closer now and realizing that it wasn't a dead pheasant after all, but one made of fur fabric with some of the stuffing protruding, the very embarrassed driver sped off down the road without saying another word.

Chesil was always curious. She would investigate anything new and interesting, whether it was moving or still. On the way to and from the swimming hole, we had to pass through a large intensive dairy farm. One day, a big blue tractor was parked on the other side of the field protected from the cows by a single strand of thick electric fence wire. Chesil, still wet from the river, ran towards it. I called her frantically, but she ignored me and kept going. Nose up, sniffing the air to see whether this tractor was friend or foe, she kept running at full speed, oblivious to the wire in front of her.

It was a long way across the field and, by the time she reached it, she was too far away for me to see her in any detail. In soft focus, I saw her turn abruptly and leap into the air, then I heard a yelp and saw her trotting vigorously back across the field, head and tail low to the ground. It was months before she ran into that field again. As soon as we went through the gate to the footpath that led to the field, she would fall into line behind me, tail slightly down, ears pinned back. Luckily, she didn't hold it against all tractors as could have happened with a violent one-off learning experience such as this. She did, however, mistrust that field for several months.

Hardly anything affected Chesil and it was impressive to see what the pain of an unexpected electric shock could do. Sadly, there are training collars available that deliver an electric shock to the dog's neck at the press of a button. The dog cannot see where the shock comes from, or predict when the next one might occur. I've seen demonstrations in the USA and the dogs wearing such collars look miserable. They might be doing the required actions and responding appropriately, but they look tense and apprehensive, and it is terrible to imagine what they must have gone through to learn what was required. When Chesil had made me frustrated beyond endurance with her refusal to obey instructions, I would have dearly loved to have a button to press to make her do as she was told, but I knew that this quick-fix approach causes lasting damage to a dog's psyche and that a dog abused in this way would never fully trust again. That these devices are openly displayed for sale in many countries is a sad and frightening reminder of the violence and suffering ordinary people are prepared to use to achieve their goals.

Shock collars are often used to attempt a cure for dogs that chase sheep. They may provide a quick fix, but not a lasting cure since the desire to chase is still there and, once the memory of the shock has dimmed, it becomes too strong to resist. During the first year we had Chesil, we lived in the Cotswolds and virtually every field we walked through contained sheep. Being hilly, the sheep wouldn't necessarily be visible at first, but then several of them would pop up unexpectedly and temptingly from behind a mound.

When Chesil first came to live with us, Grant was adamant that she wasn't a sheep-chaser. 'She's never chased a sheep in her life, he said, 'It's horses she doesn't like.' Actually, it turned out to be the other way round and it was sheer lack of opportunity on her walks in the past that had made Grant's statement about sheep true. 'She needs to be on the lead,' I cautioned, as we went into a field where sheep were peacefully grazing, spotting her interest in them immediately.

I had carefully socialized Spider with sheep at an early age, taking him to meet a friend's two friendly hand-reared lambs so that he could get used to them and not learn to chase them. Having grown up with the farm dogs, the sheep had no fear of Spider and so he wandered around behind them trying to lick their bottoms. Frequent, steady walks at heel in fields with sheep when he was young had taught him how to behave well around them. Now that he was grown, he showed no interest in sheep and was content to chase his ball instead. Chesil, unfortunately, had not had such a thorough upbringing.

'She's okay with me,' Grant said, ordering Chesil to heel. On our first walk through this field, all was well. I didn't like the way Chesil stared longingly in the direction of the sheep, but she remained glued to Grant's side as he kept reminding her to stay with him. The sheer force of his personality, together with the prospect of the occasional treat that he slipped her from his pocket, kept her with him.

On the return journey, the sheep were some distance away and Spider was playing with his ball. Chesil hadn't reached the stage where she had learnt to join in with play, but she was excited by Spider's movement and ran forward to chase him as he ran for his ball. It was my mistake for luring her away from Grant, but I thought he had her focused on him and under control. Instead, because she was so good at walking to heel on the first pass across the field, and because the sheep were now further away, Grant had relaxed and was content to have her somewhere close.

Then, in an instant, she was gone. Immediately Grant shouted for her to come, but she kept running, veering off from Spider towards the sheep that she had been eyeing earlier. Now we were both shouting. We were terrified of her injuring or scaring the sheep, and of her being spotted by the farmer. I'd kept sheep in the past and knew how sensitive they were. It wasn't funny for them to be chased by a strange dog. Spider returned immediately, worried by our shouts, but Chesil kept on running up the field. The sheep, still a long distance away, saw her coming and started to run for the top of the hill.

Chesil had a morbid fear of being left alone, probably because it happened too often and for too long when she was a young puppy, and she would panic if she lost sight of us on a walk. I'd accidently got separated from her once and, when I ran to where she had been, I could see her racing for home as if her tail were on fire. On that occasion, I had called her and she had stopped in her tracks, racing back to be with me, panicked and breathless that she had nearly lost me. I knew that our best way of getting her back was to head, at speed, for the gate, calling in happy voices to let her know we were heading for home. Chasing her would only add to the game and her sense of security that the other members of her family were joining in. However, getting Grant to agree to that course of action was, I knew, more than my limited powers of persuasion or kudos as a dog expert could manage. So he started running towards her, and I walked slowly towards the gate with Spider, caught between my original plan and my desire to help Grant get her back.

Fortunately for all concerned, it was a long hill with a steep incline. Chesil was still grossly overweight and unfit. It was a hot evening and she had already been on a lengthy walk. Long before she reached the sheep I could see her tiring. Her sudden burst of speed was quickly spent and, quite soon she gave in and stopped, panting like a train. Grant was closer to her now and called her. She turned happily and started trotting down the hill without a care in the world. When she got to him, he grabbed her collar and started to tell her off, all his pent-up frustrations at not being able to stop her earlier driving him into a long tirade of scolding. When he'd finished and we headed for the gate, Chesil was now on a lead, tail low, in disgrace again.

Slightly annoyed that he hadn't complied with my earlier suggestion to have her on a lead in a field of sheep, but not wishing to say 'I told you so', I said, 'You should have praised her for coming when called,' hoping to salvage something out of the evening even though we were both now feeling annoyed, upset and disappointed with Chesil once again. Grant looked at me, incredulous that I could say something that seemed to be so totally against his reasoning. The rest of the walk was taken up with me explaining how, with no words to link the 'punishment' to the 'crime', there is no point telling dogs off unless you can catch them in the act, or, better still, as they are about to do something wrong. His scolding when she returned had only served to make her less likely to return in the future, and, in a million years of such training, she would never be able to link his telling off with the enjoyment she'd just had in trying to reach the sheep. It would have been nice to have had someone to blame the incident on, or to blame Chesil for being so naughty, but, despite our strong emotions, we knew, logically, that we had to just let them fade away in their own time and learn from the experience. We were getting good at knowing how long these negative emotions would take to dissipate, but, fortunately, it was one of the last times that we had a really bad experience with Chesil on a walk.

After that incident, we were very careful in the fields and she remained on the lead wherever there was a possibility that sheep would appear. Eventually, once ball-chasing became a great new game, all thoughts of sheep-chasing were forgotten. We had done quite a lot of work with her with sheep before then and after our bad experience with them – walking quietly through them, correcting her when she looked their way, and praising her and offering occasional treats when she didn't – gradually habituating her to their presence and letting her know that the acceptable response was to ignore them. This, together with giving her an outlet for her desire to chase, made her quite reliable. Although I wouldn't risk having her off the lead with sheep close by, if sheep were the other side of the fence and she headed towards them, I could entice her back with a ball, making sure I was ready to throw it in the opposite direction when she came. Gradually, we became more relaxed with her as she became more obedient and, apart from enjoying eating what the sheep left behind, she began to take no notice of them even if they were relatively close.

At times when Chesil was so naughty, such as when she tried to chase the sheep, it was tempting to resort to punishment to try to stop her doing it again, or just to vent our feelings of annoyance and upset that her behaviour had caused us. However, I knew from my many years of working with dogs that rather than solving problems, punishment often creates a few more that you weren't expecting. I also knew from my childhood, that punishment doesn't teach you what you are supposed to do instead; it simply flattens your spirit and causes you to bitterly resent the person who is doing the punishing.

I was the sensitive child and my relationship with my parents had left me wary of being criticized and getting into trouble. Although my mother loved me, she was quick to be cross with me, punishing me if she got really angry, leaving me crying in my bedroom at the unfairness of it all.

This left me with a hatred of punishment and negative training methods that have shaped my whole life with dogs. If I hated it so much, how must they feel when they don't even speak our language? I often saw and felt extremely sorry for dogs with angry owners, who were yelling at them and yanking them about by their collars. I knew the dogs were trying to please, but just didn't understand what their owners wanted. I knew there had to be a better way than punishment and yelling. In my work with puppies and through tutors in the Puppy School, we spend a long time giving owners alternative, positive solutions for training and behavioural problems, so that working out how to make the puppy want to do the right thing becomes second nature, instead of resorting to force and aggression. It takes a long time to go against the discipline methods people have often learnt from their own parents, but it's worth it when you see the results in confident, well-behaved puppies.

Ironically, although my mother was sometimes so angry with me, it was from her that I learnt most about compassion, especially towards animals. She would scoop up bumble bees that hit the window in the summer, keeping them safe in a matchbox until they had recovered, or rescue baby birds that had fallen out of a nest and patiently feed them until they were well enough to fly away. All creatures great and small received care at our door if they needed help, and people in the village frequently brought round injured wildlife in need of attention.

I adored my father because he was extremely kind and good natured. I would have done anything for him. He never needed to be cross as his disapproval was enough to have me in tears, and on the rare occasions that he did shout, I felt my world had ended. I learnt from him the power of a good social relationship when it comes to controlling behaviour in young animals, and how important patient, kind teaching is if you want someone to learn quickly.

From both of my parents, and also from all of those who were later in a position of power over me, from teachers through to bosses when I started work, I learnt how important it is to use positive methods to teach good behaviour. I found out, first hand, how desperate it feels to be constantly rebuked, even though you are doing your best, or how happy it makes you when people you are working for show their appreciation and gratitude. I also learnt how much better life is for social animals if those at the head of the family or organization encourage and reward good behaviour instead of scolding and dwelling on that which is unwanted. I watched closely as insecure aggressive people failed to get results from colleagues and how good leaders could inspire loyalty and devotion from their employees by judicious use of reward and approval.

All of this helped to bring me to a point, early in my career, where I decided only to use positive methods for rehabilitating and training dogs. Dogs are not so different from humans in many ways and I could see, from my own work, how good the results were if you kept people on a positive path. I knew that this road was the only one to go down with Chesil, no matter what it cost us to bite back the desire we felt to take out our frustrations on her when things went wrong, and I continued to challenge myself to come up with positive solutions to problems that didn't involve the use of punishment to change her behaviour.

Chapter 12
Bad dog to good

CHESIL had a terrible fear of being in a car, having not travelled in one enough as a puppy. Now, as an adult, she would try to rip pieces out of the seats, racing from one side of the car to the other, ripping and clawing, and screaming in distress and fury. The noise was ear-splitting and the damage intolerable. So we decided we would only take her out in a travel cage in the back of Grant's old Range Rover. That way our cars would be preserved, she was distanced from us slightly so the noise was a little less deafening, and we could begin to teach her to settle on journeys.

Grant had a very nice car – a sleek, black, racing machine that encouraged him to drive too fast. It was his pride and joy, although I preferred not to travel in it if he was driving, as the fast speed scared me too much. We joked how, one day, we would have Chesil so calm that she could travel sedately on his back seat, watching the world go past calmly from a side window. I, however, doubted this as even Spider wasn't allowed on the soft leather seats, just in case he accidently dribbled or shed hairs. There was no room for Chesil in my car as it wasn't an estate and Spider and I took up all the space there was. So the only means of transporting Chesil was going to be the old Range Rover.

I had watched her carefully in the cage as we were driving and seen the tell-tale behaviour of a dog frightened by the movement and excited enough to chase anything that went past. Sheep, dogs, people; she wasn't fussy. As long as it was moving rapidly past the window, she would go for it, yelling for all she was worth. She would then spin as it passed and get ready to watch for the next one. She was both afraid and frustrated at the same time, acting on impulse, totally out of control.

Spider had been worried about car travel when he was a puppy, but his worries had internalized and he had become sick instead. I had worked with him slowly for his first year, driving carefully, stopping when he started to look queasy to allow him to recover on solid ground before putting him back into the car to try again. It had been a slow process, but it had worked and now he was content to travel anywhere and everywhere. Chesil must have had the same fears as a puppy but no one had understood this. Trying to work on this problem at the age of four-and-a-half was going to be much more difficult.

I knew that covering her cage would cut out some of this behaviour since she wouldn't be able to see anything going past. It wouldn't stop her being frightened, but it would prevent the excited chasing. However, it was mid-summer and we didn't want her to overheat so, instead, I attached a chain lead to her harness, threaded it through the bottom of the seats at the back, persuaded her to lie down with a treat, then fixed it so she couldn't get up high enough to look out of the window. I made sure that, should we have an accident and have to stop quickly, she wouldn't be hurt before she came to rest at the back of the cage. This had worked well on some short test journeys that we had made to local walking places and she was beginning to become quieter and more relaxed about travel.

In late summer, as things were beginning to settle down for us all, we decided to go to a country fair about 12 miles away and, determined to make Chesil into a dog we could take anywhere, we took her with us. With hindsight, it was all a bit too much too soon for her. All went well on the outward journey. We'd given Chesil a rubber toy stuffed with pâté and that kept her quiet. Although she was still worried by the movement of the car, she now had something to focus on. Frenzied chewing and licking noises could be heard coming from the back, but they were a lot better than the high-pitched yelps usually accompanying us. Grant and Holly thought it was a miracle cure, but I knew we were a long way from that just yet. Spider sat on the back seat with me and watched the road through the gap in the seats.

All went well at the fair. Grant, Holly, myself and the two dogs wandered around in the sunshine, all calm and relaxed, like a happy little family. The bangs coming from the clay pigeon shooting bays in the distance didn't seem to worry Chesil too much. The first house she had lived in had been struck by lightning and only Chesil was at home when the thunder and lightning exploded into the chimney and tore a big hole in the roof. Since then, unsurprisingly, she had been worried by loud noises. So we kept her at a distance from the shooting bays, not wanting to scare her and spoil the day.

The journey home was more tense since we had forgotten to take more pâté for the toy. Instead, I resorted to feeding Chesil treats through the bars of the cage when we went round a corner, over a bump or had to slow quickly. That kept her quiet most of the time but occasional yelps and barks escaped, making us cringe at their unexpectedness.

When we reached home, I opened up the tailgate and moved towards the cage door to release Chesil. She flew at the bars, lips up in a deadly snarl, screaming like a banshee, intent on delivering a bite should I go any further. Hearing the disturbance, Grant came to offer assistance. 'Stop it, Chesil,', he ordered, and moved with calm confidence to open her cage. He got the same response and was clearly shocked by her frightening aggression, worse than anything we had seen before.

I wondered if it was because she was fastened to the back so I dug around behind the cage to release her, causing yet more wild yelping. The neighbours must have wondered what we were doing to her. Still the same response when we went towards the cage door. Her lead was now free so I thought that if I could get hold of the end, we could work it towards the door and then use it to remove her from the car, whisking her out before she had time to think about being aggressive. A wire coat hanger was produced and we fiddled around for a long time, trying unsuccessfully to fish for the handle. More yelps and defence from Chesil and more frustration for us. 'Let's leave her for a while to calm down,' I suggested after many failed attempts. We opened all the car doors, as it was still warm, and went inside.

Half an hour later, we went out to try again. If anything, she seemed to have wound herself up into even more of a frenzy. I wondered if it was because she was feeling trapped in her cage. Fortunately, Grant's front garden was very secure so we shut the gates and bolted them to make sure no unsuspecting passerby would come in. Going back to the cage, I carefully slid the fastenings back, knowing that her mouth and teeth couldn't come through the bars, leaving me safe. I waited while she raved, then, during a lull, I moved carefully aside, opening the cage door as I did so. She lunged forward, free to rush out and bite me or remain inside. She chose to remain inside. We slowly walked away and went into the house, closing the door and leaving her to calm down and get out of the car in her own time.

Grant fretted about her while we waited. He is tough and uncompromising when he needs to be, but, underneath, he has a really kind nature. I loved this aspect of his character but I didn't agree, this time, that Chesil deserved our sympathy. He was worried that she wasn't happy out there all alone. I reasoned that she could come in and join us if she wanted to. He kept looking out of the window to see how she was and really wanted to go out again to try and get her to come in, where he thought she would feel better. I was happy to be away from her. She now had choices and was best left alone. I was, once again, regretting the disruption she caused to our lives, unreasonably cross at how she was repaying us when we had taken her on a nice day out. I needed time to cool down and remember that she was just a dog with issues and that it wasn't surprising that there were still times, like this one, even after we had worked so hard with her and come so far, when, out of the blue, she would behave in a way that caused us more distress and anguish.

An hour later, she still hadn't come out. We tried rustling food packets and clanging bowls, but to no avail.

We couldn't leave her there indefinitely. So, eventually, I made the decision to use the compressed air can again to force her to leave the car. I didn't like doing it, but could see no other way out of the situation other than leaving her there until she was starving and needed to come out to survive. I tried to calculate how long this would take. Having made a rough estimate of about two days, I knew we needed to get this over with more quickly than that so we could get on with our lives.

'Come out like a good dog,' I said quietly, knowing she wouldn't understand me. But it made me feel better to say it, knowing what I was about to do. I approached closer to the cage, she flew forwards, snarling, head pressed up to the top in the open doorway, daring me to come nearer. One air blast into the space beside her was all it took. She knew, instantly, that she was defeated. Her attitude changed immediately and, with head and tail lowered, she jumped out, skirted round me and raced for the safety of the house.

Later, as we rested after a long day in front of the TV, Chesil sat with her head facing the wall, big stress lines underneath her eyes. Our big outing that day had been just too much and had sent her into meltdown. A normal day out with the family that Spider enjoyed and took in his stride was just too much for Chesil. Although very reactive, she had quite a fragile psyche underneath and we needed to take care in future not to overwhelm her again. So we resumed our smaller outings, taking Chesil out only for short excursions rather than for a whole day. She was still touchy about us approaching the cage, but I now trapped her chain lead in the door so that it was ready to pull her out with once we had got it open. I never wanted to be in a situation again where I couldn't get her out. Imagine if we had an accident.

Apart from this slight setback, Chesil was settling down nicely. Her aggressive incidents were fewer and she was getting much more responsive to instructions. About this time, Grant had to go away for a week on business so I volunteered to take her to my house for a few days to save her from the upset of going into kennels. Journeys in the car were now more frequent and less eventful, and gradually becoming less noisy as she adjusted, so I loaded her up and went home. She had been to my house before and always went straight under the table so, when we got settled, I put her bed there so she would be comfortable.

All went well for the first few days and then, unexpectedly, a small parcel was delivered through the letterbox. Spider and I were upstairs at the time in my attic office. Hearing a commotion, we went down. Chesil was standing over the parcel, her body stiff. I recognized that posture and knew it meant trouble. As I approached, a deep rumbling growl came from her chest. I had brought the can of compressed air with me for just such emergencies, but it was in the kitchen and I couldn't get past her to get it. Knowing that Chesil could be very persistent, I couldn't just wait it out and, besides, I didn't think it was healthy for her to know that, yet again, she could control the female members of a household. I remembered that I'd been given two cans of the compressed air and so I went back upstairs to see if I could find one in my office.

By the time I came back down, she had realized that the parcel contained no food and was of no value. The arousal caused by the postman's intrusion had passed and she was calm again. She had left the parcel and returned to her bed. I was pleased about that as I had been unable to locate the second can upstairs.

Spider had a box of toys by the radiator near the table and I decided not to move them when Chesil came to stay, reasoning that she would need to get used to them sooner or later and that as there were so many toys in the box, it wouldn't matter if she took some. Since Spider had already established his right to take toys that were close to Chesil, he could continue to have access to them if he wanted.

Soon after the post incident, and during the same day, I noticed that Chesil had taken out a yellow fluffy duck toy and was now hunched over it on her bed, stiff and staring at me to see if I would try to take it. I wanted her to know that it was okay to have toys here if she wanted them so I praised her warmly. She got up and came towards me with the toy firmly clenched in her jaws, growling and wagging, caught in the conflict between getting social praise and not wanting to lose her possession. I praised her and stroked her back tentatively, being careful not to get too close to the front end where her teeth and the toy were. She soon relaxed and went back to bed with her prize, not so tense now that she knew she was not in trouble for taking it.

Later that evening, I was sitting relaxing on the sofa after a long day working. The TV remote control was perched on the arm of the sofa and, as I shifted position, it fell onto the floor. The back fell open and its batteries rolled towards Chesil's bed. My home was a small cottage and there wasn't much room between the table and the sofa. The remote now lay equidistant between us. Chesil stared at it longingly.

Anyone who watches TV knows how important the remote is, so I got up to retrieve it. At about the same time, Chesil left her bed, intent on getting there first. I could tell from her silent, urgent approach that she wanted it and would fight for it. It's not very often that I lose my temper with animals but, today, Chesil was pushing me to the limit. I was providing everything she needed, putting myself out to make her feel comfortable, and now she was trying to stop me using my possessions. I was incensed.

I stepped forward quickly so I could stand either side of the remote, knowing that I wouldn't be quick enough to reach down to snatch it away from her. 'Well come on then,' I shouted as loud as I could, 'Take it if you think you can.' I knew, suddenly, that I would fight to the death to keep possession of this little grey plastic thing lying on the floor in front of me. It was a matter of principle and she had pushed me too far this time. I'm not sure what I would have done. She had big teeth and amazingly powerful jaws. I had soft hands and bare feet. I was no match for her physical power. However, something in my attitude had changed and she knew it. I was not prepared to make allowances for her behaviour anymore. This was my house and she was a guest – she damn well would behave. She looked up at me, then down at the remote, just as she had done with Spider and his toy at Grant's house. I saw her head and tail drop slightly as she made her decision, then she turned and scuttled off under the table. I picked up the pieces of the remote and the batteries and sat down, my heart rate slowly returning to normal as I put it back together again.

After that, something changed between us. I was still wary of getting bitten when she was guarding something, but she now seemed more like an unfortunate, frightened child than a belligerent, aggressive animal. I knew that, if push came to shove, she could be defeated and, once I had seen her vulnerable side, it gave me the freedom I needed to become more sympathetic towards her. Whether I changed or she did is hard to tell, but something shifted. The balance now fell more appropriately and she treated me with more respect while I, for my part, began to take more responsibility for her life, rather than leaving it all to Grant. During our week together, I wasn't just a visitor to Grant's house, but someone who looked after her properly and cared for her. Once she realized that, she changed her attitude towards me, becoming more friendly and more willing to please. Whatever it was that happened during that week, I felt we'd turned a corner and I began to feel more hopeful about our future together.

Soon after her visit to my house, I needed to call upon Chesil's services to help me with some photographs for a book I was writing. It was about useful tricks owners could teach their dogs to help around the house, such as picking up stray socks if you are carrying the washing to the machine, or fetching the lead and keys to get ready for a walk. Giving a dog a job to do is so important, especially for those bred to work. If taught using positive reinforcement and praise, dogs love to do things for their owners and it helps to use up the vast amount of mental energy that causes them such frustration when they are just required to lie around the house doing nothing. This book was to be an illustrated teaching guide for owners and I had lined up a lot of wonderful people who had been frantically teaching their dogs the various tricks.

At the 11th hour, the 'shut the door' trick dog had become ill and couldn't make the shoot. I had two days to find a replacement. Spider was already heavily involved and I knew the editors wouldn't appreciate another two pages of his photos, so I decided to see if I could teach Chesil. I went to Grant's house early to do a training session while it was quiet. First I stuck a post-it note to the palm of my hand, held it out and asked her to 'SHUT the door'. Being naturally curious, she moved towards it with her nose and when she made contact, I gave her a treat. Several tries later, she had got this concept and was happily moving all over the kitchen to touch her nose onto the post-it note to earn her treat. Normally, several sessions of this would be required to cement it in the dog's mind, but I didn't have time for this and Chesil seemed to be learning extremely fast. So far, so good.

The next, harder part, is to transfer the post-it to the door and ask for a nose touch. I held my palm with the post-it attached close to the kitchen cupboard door and asked her to 'SHUT the door'. Nose touch, treat, easy. Then I slid the post-it across to the cupboard door and asked again. She looked confused. We hadn't done enough practice with the post-it on the palm and we were trying to progress too rapidly. Frustrated at not knowing quite what I wanted her to do, she moved forward slightly, then sat back down. I rewarded her with a treat. After all, she had moved her nose closer. Enthusiastic about being rewarded, she tried again, this time touching the post-it with her nose. I went wild, treating and praising her. She ran round the kitchen, excited and happy to have made me so ecstatic.

We tried again, but she couldn't do it this time. I went back to basics and did the post-it on the palm trick again near to the cupboard door. Another try and she got it. I asked again, she pressed her nose on the post-it on the cupboard door again. And a third time. She had got it! I marvelled at her ability to learn so fast. I've taught many dogs many things over the years, but Chesil seemed to be able to work out what was required faster than any dog I've ever known. No wonder she had been so unhappy living a life where there was so little to do.

I left it there and went back later, after a cup of tea and a rest, to see if I could get her to push the door shut. Knowing how enthusiastic Chesil is and how willing she is to use brute force, I held her back from the open door with the post-it attached just long enough for her to be desperate to try. She rushed forward and the door slammed shut with a satisfying thud. We celebrated and did it a few more times to check it hadn't been a fluke.

Grant came home later and we showed him Chesil's fantastic new trick. He was amazed as he had never seen a dog shut a door – it was one of the few things I hadn't bothered to teach Spider. After a few successful attempts, I removed the post-it. She knew what to do now. Grant was so impressed and proud of his dog for learning so quickly. Being someone who doesn't like to sit on the sidelines and watch, he wanted to see if she could do it for him. She could. 'Chesil, you are so clever,' he told her as he looked lovingly into her eyes. She sat, looking up at him, wagging her tail, very happy to be the centre of everyone's attention. Later, it was to become the one thing that she could do that Spider could not and it was displayed to all our friends or anyone who happened to be standing in the kitchen.

Shutting the door on command is not an easy trick. It usually takes a week of careful training with most dogs. Chesil had taken just four sessions in less than a few hours. Sure enough, two days later when the photographs for the book were taken, Chesil performed as if she had been doing it all her life, again and again, until the photographer had just the right angle. After this, the editor decided it would be more impressive to have a shot of the front door being shut. We had only worked with small kitchen doors, not large, heavy ones. I had also only taught her this trick in the kitchen and most dogs need to be taught a newly learned response again, from scratch, once you move location. I wasn't sure she could do it without further training and was hesitant. 'Why don't we try?' said the editor, so they set up their lights in the hall.

We left the door ajar, I held her at the far end of the hall, goading her into excitement by letting her move forward slightly then holding her back. 'SHUT the door, Chesil,' I said loudly, releasing her. She charged down the hall and bulldozed the door shut. We all heard the satisfying click of the shutter just before we heard the resonating boom of the heavy front door coming to rest in its frame. I was so proud. She came back to me for her treat and looked up at me, her tail waving. Suddenly she didn't seem like the dog that Grant owned that I was helping with; she now seemed more like a dog that belonged to me, part of my developing family.

Chapter 13

Doggy issues

THE first time we noticed something was wrong was in late spring, about three months after Chesil came to live at Grant's. We were all out for a walk together in the evening, strolling along a footpath that went down a long driveway towards a mansion house. The footpath then veered off over the fields before it reached its destination. The driveway was wide, with large grass verges and tall trees lining either side. It was an ideal place to walk on a warm day and lots of local dog owners used it. In the distance, I could see a man walking his black Labrador. Knowing that my large black dog can seem intimidating to other people, even though he has no malice in him, I called him to heel, rewarding him well with a treat and keeping him there with the promise of more later.

Grant did the same with Chesil. Her heelwork was impressive now and she raced to his side, pressing herself against him and looking up like a dog in a competition at

Crufts. 'She needs to be on the lead,' I said, seeing that Chesil was on the same side as the dog approaching, and knowing that this would be too much of a distraction for her to stay in place. I didn't want her to learn that she could just leave Grant's side whenever she liked after being asked to walk beside him. It was bad training. Grant, however, insisted he could keep her with him, redoubling his efforts to make her walk to heel.

Having had no previous problems with Chesil and other dogs and seeing, now that we were closer, that this dog looked easy-going, carrying his ball with his tail relaxed and waving, I didn't insist. I slipped my hand in Spider's collar as we got nearer, just in case the temptation to investigate the other dog got too much. As we got closer, we recognized the dog-walker as the local Vicar and called our hellos. Chesil, her close connection with Grant suddenly broken, peeled off towards the Vicar's Labrador. She went up to him with interest and a nice approach. The Labrador dropped his ball to greet her in return, wagging his tail as he did so. Now that she was closer and he seemed so enthusiastic about greeting her, she seemed to think better of it and went to walk past him, glancing at the dropped ball as she did so. Seeing her look towards his ball, the Labrador quickly snatched it back up again and growled, long and low in his throat, to warn her not to take it.

She was beginning to move away when she heard the growl and saw his sudden movement out of the corner of her eye. Like a teenage boy that hears a nasty remark made about him behind his back, she turned immediately and launched her attack. She grabbed the surprised Labrador by the scruff of the neck, using her body weight to push him off balance. He was caught off guard and went down. She held on, growling and shaking him until Grant got there and dragged her off. Although we checked carefully, there wasn't a mark on him, but he looked as upset as we all felt.

After we had made our apologies, she was back on the lead. 'You should have put her on the lead earlier,', I muttered nastily, cross that I hadn't anticipated it or insisted on what I had instinctively felt was right, and let down by Chesil who had been doing so well. We had a short argument about it, both releasing the tension and disappointment we felt.

'Why did she do it?', Grant finally asked, looking for answers from his expert.

'Well, she was growled at, and, thinking she was under attack, she retaliated. She's that sort of dog,' I said. 'That's the dog you bought, she's not a sweet Springer or a forgiving Labrador. She's a dog that takes no nonsense from anyone. She has a short fuse. She's a little like you.'

'I don't go round flattening people if they do something I don't like,' he said indignantly.

'You had better training as a puppy,' I countered.

He was quiet for a while. 'Well, how do I stop her?' he asked.

I didn't know enough about her problem to answer that. 'I'm not sure,' is all I could say.

Chesil had been fine with dogs up until that point. We had met quite a few on our walks and both Spider and Chesil would greet them with a sniff, moving on afterwards to continue their walk. There had been no problems, not even with a lively Springer puppy called Freddy, who always came rushing over to see us from across the field. Chesil had been a bit growly around her ball with him once or twice, but we'd solved that problem by exchanging it for a treat when we saw him approaching and keeping it until Freddy had gone on his way.

I had noticed her, once, in the early days, looking with evil intent towards two West Highland White terriers that lived in the neighbourhood. We had been separated by a wire-mesh fence at the time, having both reached a gate at the same time from opposite approaches. All four dogs had moved to the fence to investigate each other, Spider and the Westies sniffing and wagging. Chesil had moved forward, but had stiffened. She wasn't aggressive, but I didn't like what I saw. I knew she had been in kennels and I wondered if she had learnt to kennel guard. This often happens when dogs are kept next to each other with wire between them. The frustration and stresses of kennel life can push dogs lacking in socialization into aggression with their neighbours. I wasn't sure but I kept her away from the Westies in future, keeping her back on the lead while Spider went to meet them and keep their attention until we were past.

In July, Grant had needed an operation to repair a damaged disc that was pressing against his spinal cord. This injury had been caused long ago by playing rugby and other assorted physically demanding sports, but had been exacerbated by the building of a kennel for Chesil to live in while Grant was at work. This had necessitated lifting very heavy slabs to lay a solid base, as well as mixing up concrete. Although I helped him with this, he did all the heavy work and it proved to be the final straw for his back, which was already under strain. I marvelled again at what a profound influence taking on Chesil had on our lives. With the operation booked, Holly and I were distressed, beside ourselves with worry that the operation would leave him paralyzed.

Despite our concerns, the operation went well, but a reaction to one of the pain-killing drugs caused an emergency situation where Grant was raced back to hospital in an ambulance. I was frantic and Holly was distraught and began to talk non-stop again. Spider developed a 'hot spot', a patch of infected skin, which he had never had before but was well known for being something that occurs in dogs during times of stress.

We were too busy to notice how Chesil was taking it, but I expect she felt the pressure, too, as any social animal living so closely with its humans would do. It was a very worrying time for us all.

At first, Grant needed constant nursing so I stayed at his house to look after him. Eventually, he was well enough for me to go back to my office at home to catch up on some work there. So, early one morning, I was about to leave his house to go home, laden down with my computer bags, books and other bits and pieces. Despite taking her for a good walk earlier, I could feel Chesil pressing against my leg to get out of the front door. Normally, I'm good at keeping dogs behind doors, but I wasn't paying too much attention on this morning, being preoccupied with whether I had done enough for Grant before I left and whether I had everything I needed with me. Chesil would reliably come back when called now and I knew I could get her in again if I needed to. So, rather than stop, now that I was loaded up, I opened the door a bit wider to get everything out of the doorway at once, and Chesil slipped through.

Just at that moment, an elderly woman began walking across the gateway with a small Border Terrier on a lead. With two stone walls on either side, we hadn't seen her until she began to cross the gateway, and she appeared suddenly. Chesil, already excited at the thought of escaping into the front garden, raced forward. I saw her attitude change from happy elation at getting free to deadly earnest as she ran towards the dog. Seeing her intention, I dropped everything immediately and ran as fast as I could towards her.

By the time I caught up with her, she had the Border Terrier pinned to the ground and was shaking it like a rat. The terrier was screaming in terror. I grabbed her and heaved her off, shouting at her to stop. She stopped fighting immediately and looked chastened.

'I'm so sorry,' I said. 'She's a rescue dog, and we haven't had her long. She's never done that before,' I added, hoping to absolve myself of some of the tremendous guilt I was feeling for having been stupid enough to let her out. The poor Terrier was shaking and so was her owner. 'Let me put her away and then we can make sure your dog is alright,' I said, hoping to make things better.

'No, it's okay, we're alright,' said the very shocked owner, and she began walking away.

I rushed back to the house, dragging Chesil by the collar and cursing her loudly. I ran up the stairs to reassure Grant, who I knew would have heard the commotion and been worried. Then I rushed out, hurriedly picked up my things and got in the car, hoping to catch the owner before she got too far. Sure enough, she hadn't got too far along the road and I pulled alongside and got out. 'Is she okay?' I asked, bending down to stroke the dog.

'Yes, she seems to be,' she said.

She was a very shy, reserved person and clearly didn't want to talk. I looked carefully around the Terrier's neck, but could find no blood or sore places. Despite that, I knew both he and his owner would carry a lasting mental scar from the trauma of an unprovoked attack. They would always think about it when they walked past our gateway and would wonder if Chesil was there, ready to rush out on them again. I really was very sorry this had happened, and to think it had happened when I had been in charge of Chesil, too, made me feel even worse. I'm not used to making mistakes with dogs or allowing them to hurt or to cause problems for others and I felt terrible about it. I knew now that we would need to be much more careful with her in future.

When Diane, now living in France, was told about the incident, she reminded Grant that Chesil had been attacked by two black Staffordshire Bull Terriers when she was about a year old, soon after they had moved to their new house and had started walking her in a new area. The dogs had both been on leads, but had dragged their owner forwards and had attacked Chesil, a newcomer to their patch. Although there were no major injuries, the attack must have been very frightening for Chesil, who couldn't get away from them. It had lasted for some time until the owner regained control and, in the process, Diane had sustained quite severe burns on her legs from the leads as they had tangled around her. After that, Chesil had been really defensive on walks in the area and had taken to lunging and barking at other dogs across the street in an effort to keep them away. Chesil's ability to learn fast had, in this case, worked against her and she no longer trusted dogs that she met when out.

It all made sense now. Chesil's unpredictable behaviour was very predictable now that we had this vital piece of information. Living with us, all of the dogs she met were off lead and running free, and she was free herself. This situation was similar to what she had known as a puppy when her family had lived in a less-crowded place where most dogs had been free to interact in large open areas. She knew she could cope with other dogs in this environment. However, the Vicar's dog had been black and had shown some aggression to her. Even though Chesil's reaction was way out of proportion, it was now understandable given that it must have triggered such traumatic memories of the Staffie attack. And the Border Terrier at the gate was on a lead, and at the edge of Chesil's territory, a place where most dogs have the confidence to get rid of intruders.

Why hadn't anyone told me about this earlier? It was a vital piece of information that I needed to know to keep other dogs safe. I suspect Diane had thought that Grant would tell me. Grant hadn't thought to mention it, being too caught up in worrying about Chesil's aggression towards humans. I also suspect he had blanked some of it out of his mind, not wanting to think of her as aggressive. By the time Holly had arrived, we had already established a routine of walking Chesil over the fields with other dogs without incident. It was only later that I remembered the concern in Diane's eyes when we had introduced Spider and Chesil in the garden that first time. I thought she had been worried about Spider's obvious size and strength being too much for Chesil. I now realized she had been worried that Chesil may have attacked Spider.

I'm familiar with people withholding information when they pass on dogs. Many years of working at rescue centres had taught me that people do this for two reasons. To make sure no one thinks badly of them, and to make sure their dog gets a new home, since no one may agree to take it on if they are given the full facts. The consequence of this is that more dogs or people get bitten or traumatized while the rescue centre staff or new owner finds out about the problem. In Chesil's case, no one had deliberately concealed the truth but, somehow, critical information had not been passed on to me. The terrible fright that Chesil had given to the elderly lady and her Border Terrier had been a direct result of this.

Now that we knew, we could be more careful with her. We began to avoid other dogs she didn't know, mindful of her aggression if they showed any signs that may have triggered distant memories for Chesil. She was getting very responsive to recall cues now so it was not difficult to watch out for other dogs and call her back, or keep her on a lead in places where other dogs may suddenly spring into view. Spider could always be sent on ahead to intercept free dogs if they looked friendly and stop them from approaching Chesil, who was now on a lead. This allowed her to relax and we could keep her attention with a treat, turning her away from the other dog and getting her to sit. In this position, she was, effectively, turned off and most dogs would leave us alone.

We managed her very well until one day in late autumn when Grant had got up early in semi-darkness to walk her before work. At that time of the morning, only local dogs were on the field and Chesil was familiar with them all, so there was nothing to worry about. They usually greeted each other by sniffing and then went on their way. Owners normally stumbled past each other in the gloom, grunting a 'Morning!' and moving swiftly on to get the exercise over with.

One owner who frequented these morning walks had a beautiful errant yellow Labrador-Cross, fresh out of rescue, who had not yet learnt to come back when called. He was lovely with dogs and people, and Chesil got on with him really well. His owner could frequently be heard yelling at him to come back while his dog wandered happily in the opposite direction. On this morning, the owner needed to be somewhere early and so, very unusually, he had put his dog on a lead to make sure there was no chance of a protracted wait for him to return. It was foggy that morning and Grant and Chesil were meandering across the field when dog and owner passed by close behind them. Grant didn't see them but Chesil did. She also saw the lead. She flew at the dog, a dog she greeted happily and ran around with every morning with no trouble, grabbing him by the neck and shaking him in her usual style. Grant was on her in seconds, but not before she had given everyone a nasty scare and torn a piece of skin out of the Labrador's ear. It was a very bad start to the day.

Knowing there were always going to be incidents like this, no matter how careful we were, we considered our options. They were euthanasia, rehabilitation, or muzzling and management. Grant wouldn't entertain any talk of euthanasia. He argued that he'd known dogs a lot worse that lived into old age and I had to admit that I had too. Chesil's 'crimes', although shocking and traumatic for all concerned, didn't seem serious enough for a one-way trip to the vet. She wasn't actually causing any injuries and, for most of the time, she would run round very happily with other dogs without any incidents.

Rehabilitation was an option but not an easy one. I was willing to work at it, but I knew that with a personality like hers, she would always have a propensity to suddenly flip into her pattern of self-defence if she felt sufficiently threatened. I had successfully rehabilitated Beau who had an aggression problem with other dogs, but he was a different character. He wanted to stay out of trouble whenever possible. Once I had taught him that he was safe if he came to me, he would run to me whenever dogs became too much for him, allowing me to deal with them while he waited patiently for the treats that he knew would come later. After being rehabilitated, Beau was once bitten on the bottom by a German Shepherd that had reached out and grabbed him as he went past. Preferring to think of treats, he had shot round the other side of me, then sat, looking up plaintively, rather than pile into the other dog and fight. I couldn't see Chesil ever doing this. She would have launched into retaliation without even thinking about it. I knew a rehabilitation plan would take an enormous amount of time and would have limited success since she would never be trusted completely if other dogs tried to bully her. However, it was worth doing even if it only meant that she would be relaxed around dogs on leads that meant her no harm.

We considered a muzzle but we knew that if she hit a dog at speed wearing a muzzle, it would hurt just as much as, and possibly do more damage than, if she grabbed them. She wasn't biting hard enough to break the skin so a muzzle had limited use anyway. Quite a lot of the trauma of a dog attack is the sheer fright and mental angst it causes. I knew a muzzle wouldn't stop that either. The other problem with muzzling was that it would stop her from chasing balls and exercising properly, raising her frustration levels and making it more likely she would have problems with dogs more often. So a muzzle, alone, wasn't a useful proposition.

So, for now, we opted for a more careful management programme. She was kept on the lead much more, only being allowed off when we were absolutely certain that no other dogs were around. Given our location and our love of walking in the country, it was easy to find walks that no one else used or choose times of the day that were less popular for dog walkers.

A few months later, I was asked to take a journalist and photographer on my favourite walk for a popular dog magazine. The idea was that they would photograph me taking my dogs on this walk and write it up, with a map, so that others could do it too. We set off and all went well. I let Chesil off on the footpath where she had the previous experience with the electric fence, but she was over this by now and happily scampered off. I noticed the gate at the far end of the footpath opening and an owner with a medium-sized black dog appeared. I knew this dog and it hated other dogs. The owner always held him up on a short lead to stop him lunging, causing him even more concern as he was now helpless, and we usually gave him a wide berth. I knew it wouldn't look good if the 'dog expert' allowed her dog to get into a fight, so I called Chesil loudly and with as much authority as I could muster. She turned immediately, even though she saw the dog in the distance, and raced towards me, eager for the treat in my pocket. She sat smartly and I clipped on the lead, thankful for all the hours of training we had put in previously.

We moved to the side of the path, and I got Spider to sit on my other side so he was under control too. The path was wide at this point and the owner went past easily, her dog spluttering and choking as she held him short and tight against her. My dogs sat like perfect angels, patiently waiting until he was past. The photographer got some good shots and we moved on. I kept Chesil on the lead until we were in the next field in case she doubled back and brought us shame, but the rest of the walk went well and we returned home triumphant.

I knew that a time would come when I would need to do a full rehabilitation programme with Chesil to make up for the terrible experience she had when the two Staffies had attacked, but it wasn't easy to do when I wasn't actually living with her. There never seemed to be time to contemplate it with our hectic days. I knew it wouldn't be easy and it would need the help of some special friends with their dogs, but it would bring about improvement. I even consulted my friend and previous work colleague, Ryan Neile, a brilliant dog behaviourist, still working for the Blue Cross, whose opinion I really valued. Ryan had daily hands-on experience of dealing with difficult dogs and he had been having some great success with dogs that didn't like other dogs. We worked out a programme together, but I didn't get time to implement it. For now, it went on hold while we concentrated on different priorities.

Chapter 14

Moving on

BY October, things were settling down nicely. Chesil was more relaxed and was learning how to be a good dog. Holly was becoming calmer and was concentrating on her A-levels at college. Grant and I were recovering after a turbulent nine months when we had wrestled with all the problems a difficult dog and troubled teenager could throw at us, as well as a major operation, and we were getting on well.

So well, in fact, that it led to a very big surprise for me one day in late November. We were at the Puppy School conference in Devon with all the tutors and their partners, and were staying in a small hotel and its outlying cottages. At the end of a long day of talks and discussion with the tutors, I was just wrapping up the day and thanking the speakers when I noticed Grant coming in at the back of the room. He started to walk to the front of the room and, surprised by his boldness, I asked him to wait a moment as I hadn't finished. He didn't stop and retreat as I expected, but kept approaching until he was beside me and facing the audience. I had stopped speaking by now and turned to him to find out why he was there. He said, 'I wanted to say something.' Now this really worried me. I didn't know what he was about to say, but I knew I didn't want him to embarrass me in front of my tutors so I tried to get past him to leave the room, reasoning that he couldn't do so if I wasn't there.

Grant is strong and I suddenly found myself held fast so I couldn't move away from him. This was really unusual behaviour for Grant. Once I had given up trying to leave, he held out a blue velvet box containing a beautiful diamond ring, and said, 'I wanted to ask you if you would marry me?' I was temporarily speechless, looking from him to the tutors and back again.

The proposal didn't come completely out of the blue, although I hadn't expected it to happen in front of dozens of people at the conference. All through the summer, at times we were alone together, Grant had started to make vague references to wedding dresses and being married. Such comments used to have me wrestling with a host of emotions all at once. Cleverly, he had kept the comments coming and by the time he proposed, I was used to the idea and looking forward to the wedding. I could see myself happily spending the rest of my life with him, even if he did have a crazy dog and a teenager.

'Yes,' I said and the audience went wild, clapping and cheering.

The rest of our lives together promised to be easy after what we had just lived through. We joked about worldly goods and I said I would like his fast car and his daughter, but he could keep his stinky old dog. He pretended to be wounded, saying that wasn't very nice and I agreed. She wasn't a bad dog now, as well as a lot less smelly, and there were fewer incidents. I knew Chesil came as part of the package and she would be a lot easier to manage once I lived with her properly.

After commuting every evening and weekend to Grant's house for nearly a year and a half, I'd grown tired of packing and loading up the car. We agreed that finding a house that we could all live in comfortably was a bigger priority than the wedding so we both put our houses on the market. Grant sold his house first and I found a buyer for mine a few weeks later. After a short search, we found a huge old house in need of renovation in Gloucestershire. I wasn't keen on the idea of renovating, but the house came with five acres of land which would be perfect for my horse, Zac, a lovely Arabian who I'd owned for ten years. After years of keeping him on other people's land, I would be able to wake up every morning and see him from the bedroom window. The house, although old, was big and rangy and I knew we would all be able to fit in together without falling over each other. We made an offer and it was accepted.

The relative completion dates meant that Grant and Chesil would come to live with me for six weeks. Holly went to live with a friend during this time as there was no room left in my tiny cottage. We were bursting at the seams with dogs, clothes, bags and boxes. I was trying to pack up my house, where I had lived for 15 years, but we were also trying to live there and it was chaos. Our stress levels were high as we coped with all the upheaval. Grant was also in the process of changing jobs, stressful in its own right, without living out of suitcases and having most of your possessions packed up and in storage. It wasn't an easy time, especially when the phone company cut us off three weeks early, leaving us with limited communication with the outside world. The tension had a knock-on effect on the dogs' stress levels, as always happens in a family. Spider could cope as he was well balanced and seemed to know that it was just a rough patch. Chesil, who had now moved house for the fourth time in her short life, found it more difficult and spent a lot of time under the table out of the way.

One Saturday just before we moved into our new house, Grant had gone out for the day and I decided to go and ride my horse. I took Spider and we left, leaving Chesil some much-needed space to relax and unwind. After a lovely, long, relaxing ride in the sunshine, Spider and I arrived back at my house. Grant's car wasn't there so I knew he wasn't back yet. Walking up to the front door, which had big glass panels with a net curtain across it, I could make out the shape of Chesil, barking to guard the house as usual. As I got my keys ready to put in the lock, picking through them to find the right one, I noticed that Chesil's bark was different to her normal 'Keep out, this is my house' bark. It was more excited, with a quick, high panicky edge to it. She sounded more like she did when she was guarding a bone or something she had found. I was interested to see what was the matter with her, so I opened the door a fraction. The door was stiff and stuck at a point where it was only open a quarter of the way. Before I could push it open further, Chesil had launched herself at the opening, teeth flashing, a deep blood-curdling growl coming from her throat. She blocked the door with her big solid body and I knew I could go no further without risking her rushing out to bite me.

Entrances are important places for dogs, just as they are for people. Most people would fight an intruder on the doorstep who was trying to get into their home, whereas they wouldn't if they came downstairs to find the intruder already sitting on their sofa. Dogs seem to have the same sense of territory and, for some breeds, protecting the boundaries is a very strong instinct. Many strangers get bitten at front doorways or front gates, even if they had intended no harm. Fearful dogs worry they are being invaded and try to defend their property before it's too late. So I knew better than to just kick the door open and walk in. I closed the door to think and recover from the shock of not being able to get into my own home for the first time in 15 years.

For a moment, I couldn't work out why Chesil was doing this. Why would she suddenly start to defend the house from me? We had not left her alone for so long in my house before but, even so, it didn't explain why she was reacting this badly. The barking had subsided by now so I opened the door again to see if I got the same response. Chesil exploded into an aggressive rage. I made little feints with the door, trying to work out just how far she would go. She positioned herself so that I could see her face, nose wrinkled in a snarl, still growling loudly, saliva now dripping from her lower jaw. I decided she was willing to go all the way.

At a slight loss to know what to do, I closed the door again. Spider was right behind me so I stood back a bit to let him see and opened the door a fraction. I was half hoping he would take her on and put an end to it as he had done all those months ago over the toy, but he turned away as if suddenly becoming interested in something out near the road and I knew he didn't want to get involved. So I phoned Grant to find out how far away he was and to see if he could come home and help.

'Listen to this,' I said, opening the door a fraction. Loud growling ensued. I closed the door. I opened it again, loud growling again, I closed it. Grant was too far away to help so I would have to solve it myself. It had been a long ride and I was desperate to get inside to rest and eat, so I was hoping I would be able to resolve the problem quickly.

While I had been on the phone, I was looking down and noticed a pair of Grant's boots inside the house by the front door. So that's what Chesil was guarding! She had never done it before, but these were strange times for her. Perhaps these were the only thing that smelt of security in her long time without us in the house. Whatever the reason, I knew I had to get those out of there and then she would be okay.

I found a short stick in the front garden, strong enough to hook a boot out with, and I opened the door to try. I could hook the boot with no problem but I couldn't get it out of the door without Chesil's head, and then her body, coming too. As the boot was coming out, so was she. I realized that I would soon have one boot in the house, and one boot in the porch, complete with growling, guarding dog loose in the front garden. The front garden was very small and so the road was close by. She would be out of control and potentially dangerous to passers-by, so I poked the boot back into the house and shut the door to think of another plan.

Suddenly, the solution came to me. Her lead was on a hook high up, but just inside the door. I opened the door slowly and slipped my hand through. It was high enough up for her not to be aggressive towards it. I felt for the lead and lifted it off its hook, bringing it out triumphantly. 'Want to come for a walkies?" I asked her. At the mention of the magic word in its usual happy tone, complete with visual cue in the form of the lead, Chesil transformed into a different dog. She became relaxed again, her tail waving excitedly, smiling with all thoughts of aggression gone. I opened the door wide enough for her to come through and she trotted out. I clipped on her lead and tied her to the gate while I picked up the boots. By the time I had brought her back in, she was back to normal and pleased to have us home.

I marvelled at the way dogs can switch from one mode to another. She had been in deadly earnest to protect something at all costs one minute and then all thoughts of that forgotten the next. I'm sure protecting the boots by the door had seemed very important to her a few minutes ago, but now that was all over and she was content to be a normal dog again. I put the boots back down on the floor in the same place to test what would happen. She never guarded them again.

We moved into our new house soon after and suddenly felt set free as we revelled in the big open spaces. Holly joined us and we began to unpack and make the house a home. The dogs galloped around the garden together, free to be able to do so whenever they wanted now that we could leave all the doors open without worrying about them getting onto the road. Grant and I moved possessions from one place to another, out of boxes, into other boxes, into different rooms. We tidied and mended, and painted and cleaned.

Grant had left his old job and then had a one-month gap before he started another as the Managing Director of another company, so we had four weeks to get the house in some sort of order. We were on the move constantly and where we went, the dogs followed. They didn't have to, but they liked to be with us so they were always on the move too. This was fine for Spider, who has always been an active dog. As a puppy, I would take him out and about often throughout the day and he was used to a life that involved lots of movement. It was different for Chesil. She had lived a very sedentary life until now, and then the past year in a kennel for most of the day. Now, instead of sleeping, she was walking, then lying down and getting up again. Even though she was now slim and fitter after a summer of lots of walks and plenty of swimming, the strain was beginning to show and by the end of the day she was very tired indeed. During that month she was a very good dog. She didn't steal anything, she didn't guard anything. We decided it was because she was just too tired.

While Grant was still at home, we made an appointment with the vets to have Chesil vaccinated. She was loaded into the old Range Rover at the allotted time but, unfortunately, the battery had gone flat so we all had to get out again. With no time left to charge the battery, we decided to take her in my car, with me in the back to prevent her biting or scratching the seats and Grant driving. Once in the back, Chesil was frantic. I held her so that she couldn't move around too much and asked her to lie down. She knew this cue very well now and would flatten down, seize the treat and then bounce back up again to worry about the world going past.

Dogs that are anxious often snatch food, biting at fingers in their haste to get what they need to feel better, their minds on what they are worrying about. They don't mean to nip your fingers, but they are just careless about how they are using their teeth at that moment in time. I tried holding onto the food treat to keep her down and occupied for longer, but the combination of her strong jaws and her insistent nipping hurt my fingers.

I gave the treats a rest for a while and she began to chew her lead, desperate to put something in her mouth to relieve the feeling of tension she was experiencing. Dogs under stress often look for something to put in their mouths, whether it is a lead or clothing, in the same way that humans bite their nails or chew their lips or hair. I'd noticed she always bit at the bars of her cage when she travelled in the other car. She didn't look as if she was trying to get out; it just seemed to be a way to take her mind off the anxiety. This is why we gave her a strong toy stuffed with pâté when we travelled anywhere, but it was too messy for my lap and, in our rush to find alternative transport, I'd forgotten to bring some rawhide chews as a substitute.

So I went back to using treats, trying to cover them completely with my hand at first, so she had to use her nose to try to unearth them. She was calming a little now that we were on a straight road and so it was easier. At least she wasn't barking when she was looking for treats and it was a relatively peaceful, and mercifully short, journey.

Grant had said Chesil was well-behaved at the vets. This surprised me since she wasn't very confident about people handling her in everyday life, and vets usually see an exaggerated form of any problem a dog has if it is anxious about being at the surgery. What I think Grant meant was that she had never, until now, bitten anyone at the vets. Chesil had previously been treated for cancer of the mouth and had lost one canine as a result, although this didn't stop her having an impressive set of teeth when she flashed them. So she was used to the vets and the vets were used to her. I noticed the word CAUTION! in big red letters on the top of Chesil's computer screen notes.

We were called into the consulting room by one of the practice partners, a young, tall, confident vet who was both sensible and intelligent. He greeted Chesil as we walked in, holding out his hands at her head level as she went towards him. She rushed forward, keen to get to him but also very worried about what he might do to her, caught in the ambivalence of not knowing whether to be pleased to see him or scared about what he would do. She became very still and I worried for his safety. She squatted and urinated, a big puddle spreading out on the clean surgery floor.

I pulled her away while he cleaned up, apologizing but knowing that he must be used to it. Dogs often urinate when they are feeling overwhelmed by the presence of another stronger creature; in the same way puppies urinate to appease an older animal and show they are no threat. I'd not seen this behaviour in Chesil before but here, at the vets, she would have, previously, been totally out of control. Muzzled and held down for treatment, she knew they had got the better of her many times before and so had no confidence in her abilities to defend herself. It was interesting to see how different she was with these humans compared with those she lived with.

The vet went out and came back holding a syringe containing Chesil's vaccination. He approached her and knelt beside her. She went very still and I have to say that I admired his courage for continuing with the procedure.

Had it been me, I would have insisted on a muzzle, but he picked up some skin on her neck and gently pushed in the needle. Her head swung round, eyes wild as he did so, but he was well-practised and there was no pain. He was gone, as calmly and confidently as he came, before she had thought of what to do next.

They then took Chesil away for a blood test. I later discovered that this was routine practice for them. I didn't agree with this and wondered if they realized how stressful it was for a dog to be taken away from the people it was familiar with, while it was held still for the blood to be withdrawn. When Chesil came back into the room, she was in a state of excited distress, obviously relieved to have survived. It struck me how similar this visit was to the one she would have made had we not been able to take her on, the only difference being that she wouldn't have come out alive, and I was glad she didn't know that.

While Grant went out to retrieve the forgotten vaccination certificate from the car, I apologised to the vet for Chesil being so scary. I knew he had noticed her body language and been brave enough to treat her anyway, but I didn't think it was fair that he should have to be put through this just so he could do his job. He explained that clients often got very upset if they are told their dog may be aggressive and so he tried to treat them, wherever possible, without a muzzle. I told him that, next time, I would make sure she was muzzled when she visited. She may never have bitten but, unmuzzled, there was a chance she would and the staff at the vets knew it. Once safely muzzled, they would no longer need to fear getting bitten when they treated her and may even get brave enough to do her blood tests without taking her away from us. Out in the car, I explained to Grant what I had seen when the vet had approached Chesil and how close she was to losing control. We talked it over and before we left, we took her back in and bought her a basket muzzle in the right size.

Chapter 15

Settling down

GRANT'S new job was in Devon, a very long way from our new home in Gloucestershire. He had been going through the interview process while we were in the process of moving, and when the offer came through we had a big decision to make. It was such a good job for him at this stage of his career that it was hard to turn down, but it did mean that he would be away all week and only home at weekends. Moving all of us to Devon wasn't really possible for another two years since Holly needed some continuity to complete her studies. Selling the house we had just purchased would also have been difficult and expensive. Eventually, after much deliberation, Grant decided to take the job and we agreed to see how things worked out. This meant that, for now, I wouldn't be living with Grant for most of the time but, rather, with Holly and Chesil. I had developed relationships with each but, even so, it wasn't going to be easy. I knew it was going to be a big adjustment for us all.

It wasn't until Grant left on the Sunday evening before his first day that the full implications of my new life hit. We had been so busy planning and moving, and, more recently, working to get the house ready for us all to live in, that I hadn't really considered what it would be like for him not to be there. I spent most of that evening in tears, being unable to contain my sadness at his departure. We had been together every day for a month, nest-building in our new home, and it had been lovely. Then, suddenly, he wasn't there. In my previous house, I had learnt how to cope with the loneliness that living by myself had brought and so I knew I could get used to it again, but it was still difficult. On top of that, we'd moved away from all my friends and they were now an hour's car journey away. It wasn't easy to just drop in when I was feeling lonely, and I had lots of work to catch up on so I couldn't just run off to see them every day.

Worse still, in my bleak mood, trying to recover from the loss of Grant, adjusting to life in the new house, and going back to working hard after a long rest, I had Holly and Chesil to look after. I knew I was the only adult there now and both needed more care and attention than I felt able to give. I couldn't help resenting their presence in my new world, where there was so much to be done and I was struggling with my own problems. I also knew, however, that they hadn't had any choice about their new circumstances and that they were struggling to adjust too. It wasn't their fault they had found themselves in a new place, living with someone they hardly knew, so it was up to me to bring everything together and create a home where all of us would be happy. I didn't want the job, I really hadn't considered that this was something I would have to do when I had moved from my old contented life to be with my future husband, but now there wasn't any choice. It was either grate against them selfishly as I lived in my own little world and they lived in my house, or put some effort into integrating us all into one family that lived together happily as unit. I knew I could do it with Chesil, but what did I do with an 18-year-old daughter? I didn't know, but I knew I had to try.

Life with Chesil was surprisingly easy. She was tired from our month of frantic physical effort and, like a rescue dog recovering from the stress of life in kennels, she slept for most of the time for the first few weeks. We moved her bed to the hallway so that she could be our first line of defence for any intruders. As two women living alone in a house in the middle of nowhere, we felt vulnerable at night, but we knew that it was unlikely that anyone would get past Chesil at the bottom of the stairs. Spider slept next to my bed so, we reasoned, in the unlikely event that anyone should manage to get past Chesil, Spider would be waiting for them at the top of the stairs. We should be fairly safe.

Chesil was a bit disruptive at first, barking at the slightest unfamiliar noises, but I hoped she would soon get used to them and settle down. Having our best guard dog shut in the kitchen just to get some peace and quiet when we needed her to patrol the ground floor made no sense. So we put up with the barking, calling down to her to be quiet when it went on too long, hoping that she wasn't reacting, on those occasions, to a prowler outside. After a month, she learnt what noises were normal and what were unusual and stopped barking at most things she heard. Thankfully, she gave up her regular barking at 4 am every morning when the pack of hounds across the valley woke up and started to howl. Even for us, it was an eerie noise in the darkness and we were relieved when she got used to it and gave up responding. Eventually, she barked only when something unusual caught her attention. We would then wake up and listen intently, wondering if her deep, rumbling growl needed to be taken seriously. Fortunately, she would soon go quiet, having decided it was nothing to worry about, and we would all go back to sleep, knowing that we were safe from harm for the moment.

Chesil's bed was now against the stairs and opposite my office. During the day while I worked at my computer, I could see her sleeping. When she woke up, she would come in for some fuss, pushing herself in between my desk and the chair and looking up appealingly with her big brown eyes. She was no longer alone in her kennel all day as she had been at Grant's, and this must have made a tremendous impact on her levels of stress. She finally relaxed and we gradually saw her change over time to become calmer and happier. It was hard to say if she missed Grant or not. She was certainly overjoyed to see him when he came home, as I was, but she had such a contented life during the day that I don't think she was that aware of his absence.

She also now had a very set routine with plenty of exercise, chasing balls in the fields, and going on lots of walks as we explored our new surroundings. Walks were not as restful for me now since I had to be on red alert most of the time to make sure Chesil was either on a lead or there were no dogs around. The area where we now lived was less populated than previously and so it was easier to find walks where others didn't go. Chesil's recall was now so much better as I practised every day. Since I was in charge of her feeding, I kept her much leaner than Grant, who had a tendency to feed her just a little bit extra to make up for leaving her alone all day. I always walked her before she was fed so she was hungry for the treats I was offering as a reward for coming back, and so she was now rushing back to me at top speed as soon as she heard the cue. I was also able to use toys as a reward for coming to me, calling her and then, as she raced towards me, throwing the ball in the opposite direction so she would thunder past me, running flat out to try to catch it before it went too far. Now that she had slimmed down and was fitter, she was incredibly fast! I walked her in open places where I could see dogs coming from a long way off, then I would recall her and put her on the lead so all would be well.

Our isolation from other dogs gave Spider a few problems since he now went for weeks without seeing others of his own kind, aside from Chesil. My monthly visits to Battersea to attend Trustee Board meetings for the Dogs Home gave him a chance to brush up on his social skills when I took him for a pre-meeting walk in Battersea Park. There were always lots of dogs in the park, and they were all very well socialized, meeting and greeting many dogs a day every day. I had been taking Spider there for many years without incident. Now, he started to raise his tail and hackles when he met dogs in the park, showing his insecurities and anxieties about how they might behave.

I had confidence that he would sort it out and be nice with other dogs, but I could see other owners were very worried when this huge spiky dog approached, head and body raised to give himself extra height. Although he is very large and black, there had been no problem previously as he would greet other dogs happily, relaxed and with his tail windmilling. Beaucerons have genetics that make them easily afraid of the unfamiliar and I knew that I would need to work harder to keep him socialized to avoid problems in future. So I started to take him back to places we used to walk where I knew there would be lots of dogs he knew and liked. This wasn't difficult as I liked to take him with me wherever I went, and I still had lots of business reasons to return to our old haunts during the day. So back we went, leaving Chesil at home, and, slowly, Spider's confidence in dealing with other dogs returned.

Spider and Chesil seemed to settle down completely with each other now that they lived together. There had been no fights when they both lived in my cottage for six weeks and now that we were all together, they both seemed content to be around each other. So much so that Chesil started to invite Spider to play but he never accepted. He is not a dog that plays easily with others, and I think he tried with Chesil early on and had decided she was too rough. So she had to be content with his occasional attentions when he would sniff her ears or face. She liked this and seemed to want it to continue. Rather sweetly, she would raise her paw high into the air, and point it as if asking him to do it again. This was the familiar signal she used with humans when she wanted attention. It was very pretty and worked almost every time. I knew this was not part of normal dog body language, having carefully observed thousands of dog-dog interactions, and that it was a learnt behaviour that humans had reinforced. Spider would have no idea what it meant and, sure enough, he was completely indifferent to it. Only the observing humans would sigh quietly and say 'aahh'!

We had a call from the vet to say that the routine blood test had shown that Chesil's liver enzymes were slightly raised, indicating something may be wrong. I had to take her back a few weeks later for another test, safely muzzled this time, but nothing showed up and the levels were back to normal. I suspected that the abnormality was a result of all the stress of moving house and being on the go all day, every day, for a month while Grant was at home. With more time to relax and rest, her body had healed itself and now all was well. I found myself relieved that Chesil was going to be okay and realized I was slowly assimilating her into my life and my heart.

While Chesil settled nicely into our new routine, Holly proved to be more difficult. When Grant was first working away, I went overboard, trying to provide Holly with everything she needed so she could concentrate on her school work. So I did her washing, cleaned the house and cooked for her in the evenings, fitting it in around my own work and care for the dogs. After a few weeks, I could see this plan wasn't working. I was annoyed and frustrated that while I was working so hard to help her get her homework done, she preferred to watch TV and talk to her friends on the phone.

I knew it was difficult for her, too. She now lived with me instead of her father and mother who loved her unconditionally. I was no substitute for either. I was just a person she now lived with who gave her rules, such as insisting she take out cups and plates to the kitchen when she had finished with them rather than leaving them on the side for Chesil to lick. I was even stricter than Grant had been, working hard to establish good habits from the outset in the new house. I tried to be positive and reward good behaviour, but there wasn't much to reward and I couldn't resist annoyed outbursts where I would lose it and demand she do as she was told. This brought a resentful, sullen attitude, much like Chesil had shown in the early days when we told her off. Grant was a long way away and busy with his new job. I didn't like to bother him with my issues, but my frustration had to have some outlet and I would frequently regale him with Holly's latest exploits. I didn't want him to take action as I knew that had to come from me, so I expected him just to listen. It was a hard thing for a man to do and added to his stresses. Life was really difficult for all of us.

Eventually, things came to a head. I ranted and raved at Holly, detailing all the difficulties I was facing and how I was making a huge effort and she was making none. She hung her head and cried. I felt mean but glad to get everything out in the open. I stopped looking after her and decided it was time she stood on her own two feet. I closed the door on the piles of dirty washing in her bedroom, knowing that she would do it when she needed something to wear, and I stopped cooking for her, letting her make her own dinner and look after herself. This gave me the space I needed to see that she needed help emotionally to deal with all the things she was trying to cope with. We began talking like adults instead of me treating her like a child in need of looking after. Gradually we began to make progress.

Chapter 16

Learning to trust

AS things began to settle down with my new family, I realized that Chesil hadn't had an 'incident' for a very long time. Months had passed since she had felt the need to become aggressive. Whether this was due to good management or to feeling more relaxed and happy, I wasn't sure. Perhaps it was a little of both, together with the fact that she had no energy left to be naughty as I kept her occupied with things I liked her to do instead.

Chesil's food obsession had downgraded from 'obsessed' to 'interested' without any active management on our behalf, even though I had reduced her calorie intake so that she was now the correct weight. She was much slimmer than when she first arrived. From underneath all that excess weight, a beautiful, good-looking Chesapeake had emerged that could run properly rather than only waddle. She no longer made regular forays into the kitchen to jump up at the surfaces, hunting for food. I had caught her in the act once or twice, acutely aware now of where she was and what she was up to since she had to come past the open door of my office to get to the kitchen. I had told her off and she had looked chastened, not enjoying my disapproval.

So she learnt that she could no longer sneak a quick mouthful off the surfaces in the kitchen when no one was watching as I was always watching. She learnt that I would always be paying attention and there were no times, apart from when I was asleep, that I wouldn't notice what went on in the house. As well as that, she was now content to be where we were, and where the food was not. She preferred to be with us, relaxing and getting the occasional fuss than be away from us foraging. She had plenty of opportunity to use up her desire to seek things out, use her brain to solve problems and get treats when she went out on walks. The rest of the time she was content to relax.

The field that came with our house was a smorgasbord of doggy delights, such as the entrails of a dead crow left over from a fox's dinner, the skull and ribs of a dead fox that had crawled into a bramble hedge to die, an abundance of fresh rabbit poop, or a tempting fox pooh that in the old days would once have brought on a frenzy of rolling. Chesil ignored everything, being content, instead, to sniff out rabbits to chase or to wait for a ball to be thrown.

Once, a dead bird, half-eaten by a fox proved too tempting. I saw her hunched over, chewing frantically and wondered if she would leave it if I asked her. I called and she got up, responding automatically, the pathways of cue, response and reward firmly fixed in her brain from all the rehearsal with toys we had done in the last few months. Then she remembered her dead bird. She hesitated. Then, having thought about it, she reached down, picked it up and brought it with her. She came bounding back, pleased with her prize but not worried about bringing it to me.

As she approached, I could see two legs dangling from her mouth. Despite this, I was proud of her for making the right decision to come back to me, and I praised her warmly. I was carrying the racquet that I used to hit the tennis ball, so I held it out as I would have when she brought a ball. She hesitated, wondering if I could be trusted. I brought the hand that was in my treat pocket halfway out and this made up her mind. She carefully laid the remains of the bird on the racquet and I threw her the treat, again with much praise. Then, after she had finished chewing, I held out the racquet so she could take back the revolting remains.

I was so very proud of us both. We had finally achieved a trusting and working partnership that had a very practical application. I knew now that if she found something that really wasn't good for her and would make her sick, I could get it back if I needed to. I hadn't expected to build up this level of trust with a dog as possessive as Chesil and I was really pleased to have been able to do so. We had come a long way from the days when she had eaten the rabbit skin and been sick on the cream rug.

Along one side of our property, there was a solid 6-ft high wooden fence. Behind this, lived two large dogs. They could be heard but not seen and would frequently run to the fence barking when they heard us on the other side. Chesil would race along the fence line when she heard them barking, tail and head up, bouncing on her tiptoes, ready to take them on if they appeared. Spider was alarmed, too, by these dogs he could hear but not see, and he would go into a frenzy of boundary marking, leaving a small offering of urine at nose height on every tree and shrub along the fence.

Chesil found one or two places where the rabbits had dug underneath and left a gap. I could see a whiskery face protruding slightly from next-door and a frantic barking and snarling battle would begin in the space as Chesil tried to make them back off. I was worried one of them might catch a tooth in a face, so I called her and she turned straight away and came to me, tail wagging, body relaxed. I was amazed. I hadn't expected her to come immediately, or even at all. I always keep food treats somewhere in my coat pocket so I gave her a lot of these all at once for being so responsive, a jackpot of food and praise to cement in her mind that this was a good response. My praise to her for being so good was genuine and profusive.

One day Grant and I were walking together across the field. The neighbours' dogs must have heard us talking as they started barking behind the fence. Chesil shot off towards them, her whole body alert and ready for action. Grant called her and she didn't respond. He called again, this time more crossly, with a definite threat in his voice. She continued to ignore him. I called, and she turned immediately, racing back towards me, looking up expectantly for a treat when she reached me. The tables had finally turned. Threats and intimidation didn't work, but reward-based training did. At last, we were finally getting somewhere.

Grant was disappointed that she didn't respond. I had to point out that it was me that now did most of the training and, in that particular place, I had drilled her over and over again to respond to the recall cue. If he wanted the same response, he would need to put in the effort. He would also need to remember to carry some treats with him so that he could reward good responses from her. He understood, but was always too busy to do the training. He envied my control of her, but was content for me to do it now that he was spending so much time away.

The field was a great place for training and since we were out there every day for exercise, teaching Chesil became a routine. Positive training is always fun for dogs and Chesil loved it, going into a frenzy of excitement when I put on my old green coat I used for walking. Finding new things to teach her was a challenge, but I made use of anything available such as the tree stumps that Grant left when he was thinning out our little wood. I taught Chesil to jump up and sit on them like a poor tiger in a circus. There was just enough room for her to perch her bottom on top, and if she wobbled, I would steady her until she had got her balance under control. She loved this sort of training, enjoying the stimulation of learning and the close connection with me that it brought, and was always eager to learn more. She was also inventive, throwing in new ideas, such as a quick twirl on top of the tree stump before she sat down. I could then encourage repeats of these behaviours by rewarding them and put them on cue for our next session. She didn't need treats so frequently once she learned to happily work for praise alone, but I always used treats to teach something new, so perhaps this is why she enjoyed it so much.

I taught her to lay down on cue when she was running very fast in the opposite direction. I thought this might be useful one day when she was heading towards a dog in the distance or if she was the other side of a road and a car was coming. This proved relatively easy since she already loved to throw herself into a down position when she heard the cue, tail wagging, tongue lolling, ready for the treat. It was just a matter of extending this by teaching her to do it at a distance from me, and then, later, when she was running towards me, then, eventually, when she was running away. With daily practice, it wasn't long before I could pretend to hit the ball across the field, she would race away, I would shout 'down' and she would turn and fold up on the spot, waiting there until I could hit either the ball or a treat to where she lay. I loved to give this cue, watching her to see how fast she could respond, and she never tired of trying to beat her best time, throwing herself onto the ground almost before she had finished turning. The deal was that she would go down as quickly as possible and I would get the reward to her as fast as I could.

Frequently, after I had finished praising and rewarding her, I would suddenly realize that Spider was obediently waiting for his reward and praise, having stopped and laid down when he heard the cue, too. I realized I had to be careful to remember to work with him so that he didn't feel left out, even though he knew how to do most things already.

Now that I lived with Chesil full time, I had lots of opportunities to teach her to accept things that she was worried about. I worked on her acceptance of nail- clipping, cementing the idea in her mind that, for a painless clip of her nail, she could get a treat from the pot on the windowsill just above her nose. She started actively placing her paw into my hand so I could hurry up, and we finished all her nails in record time with no wrestling.

I used a similar technique to teach her to accept being muzzled, so that we would be ready next time we needed to go to the vet. I began by putting treats into the muzzle at first so she had to put her nose in to eat them. She managed this step easily and was soon racing over to plant her face in the muzzle to get the treat. Once she could do that, I asked for a face plant but fed the treat through the side of the muzzle. We progressed until I could, eventually, feed treats with the muzzle fully tightened. When I stopped feeding treats, we praised her and told her how clever she was, as we had done when she had been carrying a toy. She was so pleased to be the centre of attention that she ran around, head up, happy to wear her muzzle and be clever. A few more sessions and she completely accepted the muzzle, wearing it without a thought as humans would wear a watch.

Spider's toy box was kept in the hall and now that we all lived together Chesil had free access to it. She wasn't that interested in the toys, except for a small, fluffy yellow duck that she often took to her bed and washed as if it were a stray puppy. She looked a little wary if I approached, but she soon learned that I wasn't interested in taking it and became more relaxed. If I called her out of her bed and into the kitchen, she was happy to give it up for a treat. I returned it afterwards so she knew she wasn't losing it forever.

Now that I was always around, it was easier to teach Holly how to cope when Chesil became possessive of things. Holly was peeling an orange in the kitchen one day and accidentally dropped a small piece of peel on the floor. Chesil went over to investigate and Holly, fearing that orange peel may be injurious to dogs, began to scold her, trying to intimidate her into moving away from it as she had learnt in the past from her parents. Chesil immediately stiffened and I could see there was going to be trouble. I quickly asked Chesil to 'fetch' and 'bring it here', as we had taught her with her toys, and she did so immediately, switching into her trained behaviour readily, seemingly happy to avoid the confrontation once she knew how to. The peel was given up and a food treat was given in exchange. Holly could see that this was a much better system and we practised, Holly throwing the orange peel onto the floor deliberately and exchanging it for a treat when it was returned. Old habits die hard and it was unlikely that Chesil would ever lose her possessiveness, but at least we all had a way to get things back from her now.

At Christmas time, my godson, Taylor, and his family came to visit. Taylor was eight years old and his sister, Hallie, was six. They have been brought up around dogs and horses, and are bright, sensible children that are unlikely to get into trouble with animals. I explained when they arrived that Chesil was friendly, but that she was possessive and not to touch her if she had found something she wanted to keep. They understood and, after initial introductions where we had been careful not to let Chesil jump up, all was well.

Not quite knowing what to buy Hallie for Christmas, I'd settled on a toy hamster in a clear plastic bubble that ran on batteries around the floor like a real pet. This was an immediate hit and she carried it everywhere. As we were going into the kitchen for lunch, the clear plastic ball slipped from her grasp and dropped onto the floor, right next to Chesil. The plastic bubble came apart into its two halves and the white hamster dropped to the floor, fortunately with its battery turned off. Quick as a flash, Hallie snatched it up, seeing that Chesil had her eye on it, but being much closer to it than she was. Chesil went over to sniff at the plastic bubble so I called her away. She came to me immediately and the rest of the toy was retrieved from the floor, and the hamster put safely back inside.

I wondered whether I had put Hallie in unnecessary danger. Some people may think I did, I wasn't sure. If Chesil was a super-fast Collie or Terrier, then perhaps it would have been different, but she was relatively slow and thoughtful in comparison. I knew that these children were sensible with animals in a way that others may not be, which lessened the risk. I knew, also, that I had been exposed to much worse when I was young and had survived intact. Risk is difficult to assess, especially when dogs and children are involved. It is possible to take all the risk away by keeping the dogs away from children, but then they miss out on all the interest and happiness they bring. As our country becomes more populated, there seems to be less and less room, and tolerance, for dogs and it will be a sad place when they are no longer welcome.

Chapter 17
Good citizen Chesil

FOUR months after he started his new job in Devon, Grant gave in his notice and came home for good, deciding that life is too short to be away from his family for most of the time. He had made a good start with the company and had left them with some positive ideas and practices, but he wanted to come home to us and start his own company instead.

Holly, the dogs and I were all really pleased with the decision. As soon as he was home, we all relaxed a little more and began to enjoy life again, instead of just getting through it. Grant was an important part of our world and we preferred him to be in it rather than many miles away for most of the week. He pulled us together as a family in a way that I couldn't do alone and I was really happy that he was back. Suddenly we seemed to have more time to dedicate to having fun rather than just working all the time.

Now that Chesil's training in the field was coming along so well, I decided I would begin training her for the Kennel Club Good Canine Citizen Awards. This would give us something to aim for and make me work at things I wouldn't otherwise have bothered with, such as teaching Chesil to stay even when I was out of sight. I had worked my previous dogs in the sport of working trials and so I was no stranger to the world of preparing dogs for a test, but I had never been involved with the Good Canine Citizen Awards, a scheme that I had heard a lot about and that was being practised at many dog-training clubs around the country.

I knew that I would need to find a club and get Chesil used to being with other dogs as all of the tests are done in groups. I asked friends and found that Janet Martineau's classes were close by. I knew of her success in working trials and that she had many years experience. Her classes were held in a field next to her house and I knew Chesil would feel more at home there than in a hall. So, one snowy day in February, we went along.

There were about five other dogs, of all shapes and sizes, in the field when we arrived but, fortunately, no black Staffies to bring back frightening memories. Even though most looked friendly, I kept my distance, backing away when they approached, explaining that Chesil was a bit scared of other dogs. She didn't look scared and I expect they wondered why I was being so protective.

Once I explained about the Staffie attack, they understood and kept their distance. Chesil soon realized that the dogs in this field were on leads and were no threat to her. She began to relax, and focus on me, the treats and the training. The class went well and, at times, I forgot to worry about the other dogs and remembered how much I enjoyed training dogs. I loved the close connection that comes from working with an animal quietly and positively. Chesil was able to do the exercises we were asked to do easily after all the training I had put in at home and she began to completely ignore the other dogs, safe in the knowledge that they weren't going to hurt her. I put her back into the car at the end and breathed a sigh of relief that it had all gone so well.

Her second lesson also went well, but on the way home the Range Rover overheated due to a lack of water and we had to stop on the side of the road for it to cool down. After a frantic phone call to Grant to find out what had gone wrong, I managed to limp it slowly back, stopping at petrol stations along the way to top up the water that was now running slowly out of the bottom of the engine. Ashamed that I had caused irreparable damage to the car by being so focused on the training session that I had forgotten to check the temperature gauge, I was grateful to Chesil for not adding to the stress by barking loudly at all the unusual stopping and starting, not to mention the hissing noises coming from under the bonnet. She managed to remain quiet and composed in her cage at the back.

I was almost home when the temperature gauge told me it was either time to stop or it was going to explode. So I stopped, gathering up Chesil's lead and getting ready to walk the rest of the way. Just at that moment, our new neighbour was driving past and he stopped and offered a lift. I looked at his brand new shiny pick-up, and wondered if Chesil would mind travelling in the back of the open truck, her ears flapping in the wind.

'Well thank you,' I said, 'but I've got my dog with me.'

'That's okay,' he said, 'there's plenty of room in the front.'

He must have seen me eyeing up the back and looking skeptical about how Chesil would cope. So I got Chesil out of the Range Rover, and hopped into his car, asking her to jump into the well of the passenger seat next to my legs. I had visions of her barking, yelping and trying to bite pieces out of the dashboard, or out of me when we started, and of me wrestling and struggling with her all the way home. Whether it was my neighbour's good driving or just that Chesil was just too tired from her training session I wasn't sure, but she sat there as demurely as a princess and was as quiet and good as she could be.

The Range Rover was never the same again after that and had to be scrapped, so Chesil's training classes came to an abrupt halt for a while. We continued to train at home and then, one week before the test, we got another car that was capable of taking Chesil and her travel cage. We had missed quite a lot of practice by now so I asked some friends to come over to help run through the tests with me. We ran through the exercises for the Bronze and Silver tests, so I could see where we needed more work, and I practised these parts several times a day leading up to the test to give Chesil the best chance to pass. The 'handling by a stranger' exercise, where the dog needs to stay still and relaxed while being physically examined, particularly needed more work. Chesil wasn't keen on this and licked her lips apprehensively, even though she knew our friends who were handling her in these practice sessions. For the next five days, Grant and I practised this every day whenever we had a moment, running our hands over her, lifting her paws, looking in her ears, eyes and mouth and then feeding a treat. Gradually she learnt to tolerate it and to look forward to the treat at the end.

On the day of the test, we arrived to find a lot of dogs on the field. There were at least 20 and all different from those that Chesil had been used to in her classes. This was a big deal for her as she usually lived quietly at home and went on walks where we saw no other dogs. Suddenly, after being driven for miles, she was being thrust into the middle of a swarm of dogs, all moving, jumping, and having fun with their owners. I took her away from the crowds to a quiet strip of grass for a while so she could calm down and rest a little after the journey. When she was ready, I brought out the toys and treats and we did a little work on her training tasks to get her focused and ready for work, hoping to take her mind off all the other dogs around her as I walked her back into the testing zone.

Her Bronze test went really well. We did have a moment early in the test when Chesil spotted someone's handbag up in a tree. It had been put there for safety out of reach of the dogs, but it was brown and furry and looked just like a cat. Thoroughly distracted, Chesil tried to make it jump down by stretching up and bouncing on her hind legs. I tried to pull her away, but she was transfixed and wouldn't pay attention. Thankfully, the other dogs were doing their exercises and by the time it was our turn again, I had got her calm and refocused. She walked beautifully to heel, came when called, stayed still for one minute when asked, was controlled at the gate and ignored all the other dogs throughout. I was justly proud when the judge handed over our rosette and certificate.

I decided we may as well go in for the Silver test on the same day since she knew all the exercises well and there was nothing, except the small entry fee, to lose. Again, Chesil was really good. She concentrated, worked well with me, did everything I asked. Then it came to the stays. The test stay was only two minutes, with me being just a short distance away so she should have been able to do it with ease. Unfortunately, we had been positioned next to a large, lively, white German Shepherd that Chesil wasn't comfortable with. On our other side was a sweet Labrador who she didn't mind, but I'd seen her looking towards the German Shepherd and her body language told me she was worried. We had been placed quite close together and suddenly I had doubts about her staying in position without me. When the judge said, 'Last command, leave your dogs,' I asked Chesil to stay. I was worried that she might follow me out so, instead of lifting up my hand and walking away as usual I left my hand down as a further signal that she should keep still. Looking back, this must have looked very like the hand signal I used to ask her to come to heel that I had been practising for the Gold award. Whether it was this signal or whether she was worried about the other dog, I'm not sure but, nonetheless, when I looked down after a few paces, she was beside me. I put her back in position and this time she stayed, but she had come out once and failed the test. The judge was very kind, but there was nothing she could do. We had missed it by a whisker.

Janet's next tests were in six month's time and, not wanting to wait so long, I looked around for someone who was doing them sooner. One of my Puppy School tutors, Nicky Brunt in Coventry, was holding tests a few weeks later. It was a long way to drive and the test was to take place in a paved area at the back of a hall in a built-up area, quite different to the fields and country that Chesil was used to. However, I thought she could cope and it was worth a try. There was only time to go to one class with Nicky before the tests, but attending this was essential to give Chesil time to become acclimatized to the venue. So a week before the tests, we travelled to Coventry for our practice session.

We arrived a little late and flustered because roadworks had blocked a road and we had to be re-routed. This time there were no cat-like handbags in trees to distract us, in fact there were no trees at all. The paved area was surrounded by buildings and many dogs, happily working with their owners, were bouncing around inside. Chesil took one look and tried to walk the other way. I let her move to a patch of grass close by while she recovered herself and then, after a bit of persuasion with a treat, she followed me in, walking nicely to heel and ignoring the other dogs.

These dogs were graduates from Nicky's puppy classes and the difference between them and the dogs from other classes was marked. They were all really friendly with each other and also had really good relationships with their owners, having been raised with only kind methods. They worked well and happily for their owners and I could see that the positive training methods were really paying off for them.

Chesil settled down well, despite the strange surroundings, and was soon ignoring the other dogs and working like she had spent all her life there. After the Silver class, Nicky ran us through the Gold test, kindly giving us time to work through all the exercises and showing how we would be tested. I knew I had a lot of work to do on certain things, particularly the two-minute out-of-sight stays and the 'controlled separation', which necessitates tying your dog and leaving it out of sight for up to five minutes. This was really difficult for Chesil, who still worried about being left alone. She was also not one for sitting there waiting for you to return and would chew through anything that tied her, setting herself free so she could come to find you. Chewing through her lead would mean instant failure.

During the week that followed, we practised Chesil's out-of-sight stays every day on our walks. I would ask her to lie down in the woods where we walked every day, tell her to stay and then walk away with Spider. We would continue until we were round the corner, where we would stand and wait. I knew this was tough for her as she was now totally alone, lost in a wood without any company. At first I would get just out of sight, then hurry back to give her treats and praise. Then I started to leave her for longer each time. If she came to find us, her little nose peeking round the corner to see if we were still there, I would take her back and lay her down again in the same place, leaving her for less time so she wouldn't be tempted to break again. I never got cross with her. I had seen plenty of people do this when training a dog to stay, thinking it would make the dog realize it couldn't move next time. Instead, it made it insecure and this insecurity gave it a greater need to run to its owner, who would become even more annoyed and so the cycle would repeat itself, until the dog learnt in spite of the bad treatment or the owner gave up. Dogs that break stays are not being naughty. They either haven't learnt what is required or don't have the confidence to stay still without their owner. I wanted Chesil to feel confident and to trust that I would return with rewards, so I knew this had to be taught slowly. Gradually, with our positive approach, she got used to the system and I was able to leave her, eventually, for five minutes, much longer than the two minutes required for the test.

A few days before the test, Grant came out walking with us. We were on our way back to the car when I realized I'd forgotten to practise Chesil's down stay. So I put her into a down and we all walked away from her. This was a big test. If she could stay put while we all walked off in the direction of home, she would be okay on the test day. I remembered the Chesil of old, who had panicked when she had thought she had lost me on a walk.

It took a lot of trust to cope with being left in a wood by herself and to know I would return. By now, I hoped she was learning that I wouldn't let her down. I chewed at my nails while we waited and five minutes seemed like one hundred. When the time was up, I raced back to her, giving her an extra handful of treats and lots of praise. We were as ready as we could be for what lay ahead on Saturday.

All the work that I had put in with Chesil for the tests was really paying off in terms of our relationship. We were now closer than we had ever been and she was much more responsive. She felt much more like one of my dogs than just a dog I lived with. She seemed to really enjoy this sense of belonging to someone and really tried hard to get things right. She stopped getting under our feet and became more cooperative, neatly turning round when asked so we could dry her back paws, and moving out of the way rather than sitting right in the middle of the doorways when we wanted to get through, like she used to. I enjoyed training her as it was easy and she learnt really quickly. Preparing for the Silver and Gold tests had helped me work really hard on refining her training and now she could concentrate and focus for a long time.

The day of the tests came and I loaded her and the sausages I had cooked the night before into the car. When we arrived, there were fewer dogs at the venue than there had been for the class, so it all seemed less daunting. The judges were very easy-going and pleasant, so we relaxed and settled into the test easily. The first exercise was to show that you could play with your dog and then get the toy back afterwards. I thought of our first experience of doing this when I had held her on a line and she had fought like a tiger. This time she played nicely with her favourite duck toy, tugging hard but then giving it up to me readily in expectation of a treat when I asked. We weren't allowed to use treats during each exercise, but she could have them afterwards, so I slipped her some pieces of sausage at the end to keep her interested.

Next there was a road walk where Chesil had to remain calm and collected while we crossed roads, walking past other dogs and avoiding pedestrians on the pavement. During her test, seeing another dog heading in her direction, she realized she would have to pass too close for comfort so, before I could stop her, she hopped over a low wall and into someone's garden to avoid it. Luckily she did this out of sight of the examiner and by the time we had emerged from behind the parked car that was shielding us, she was walking back at heel like she had never moved out of place. It was a far cry from the days when she used to pull like a train on the lead.

The vehicle control presented us with a challenge. She was good at waiting to get in as I had been taking special care to keep our new car clean, making both her and Spider wait until I had put the protective mat in place before allowing them to jump in or out. They were well schooled in this drill and Chesil knew not to let me down. More difficult was the exercise of keeping still and quiet while the examiner got into the passenger seat and the engine was started. Chesil still had a tendency to guard the car, and particularly her cage, from strangers. I held my breath when the examiner looked at her, starting the car quickly so she would see she was okay and look away. Although I saw Chesil go still as she was stared at, she didn't growl and I breathed a sigh of relief. It wasn't so long ago that you had to be careful about getting her out of the car, taking care she didn't go for your fingers when you opened the cage door, or trigger her deafening, panicky ear-splitting scream when you started the engine. I was pleased we had gradually overcome those problems so that she had been able to pass the test, and again it struck me how far we had come since she'd lived with us.

The rest of the test was uneventful. She came with me out of a big circle of other dogs as she was supposed to, off lead, happy to leave them behind and walk with me instead. She happily accepted being handled all over by the judge, something we had worked really hard with to get her ready. She didn't try to steal the judge's food when we went up for the food manners test, and, best of all, she stayed down for two minutes when I asked her, this time well away from any other dogs that may unsettle her. When the judge called our name and we went up to receive our certificate, I was again very proud of her but, this time, I was caught up in wondering if our luck would hold and we would pass the Gold test.

The Gold test was held straight afterwards. I had put her back into the car for a brief rest, but it was soon time to get her back out. A quick run on the grass and a drink and she was ready for action again. I marvelled at her staying power. This time there were only three sets of dogs and their owners being tested so there was plenty of space for her to work in without being worried about other dogs.

The heel free exercise, where the dog has to walk to heel off the lead, went well. It was easy for Chesil as she was used to practising this in the field and would stay with me wherever I walked for many minutes at a time. She had to walk close to another dog that was on the lead, which wasn't so easy. I wondered if it would trigger unwanted memories again, so I kept her attention, got ready to grab her in case she broke away, and kept walking. She stayed with me, her brown eyes looking into mine as if she knew I wouldn't lead her into trouble and I felt incredibly proud to have earned such trust. We had come a long way since her earlier days when she would attack any dog she saw on a lead, although I knew it was only a combination of the routine, the circumstance, and promise of sausage that held her there. Even so, it was a start and gave me hope for the future when we had time to work on her problems with other dogs.

The road walk and the return to my side when called from a wait were easy and she was fast and accurate. At home, I had taught her the 'sending the dog to bed' exercise on the lawn with a piece of the blanket she slept on. We had made this a game and she would race to it, throwing herself down, tongue hanging out, wagging and waiting for the treat and praise. True to form, she had learnt it in a day and even when I moved the exercise from the lawn to the middle of the field she knew what to do and raced away to throw herself on top of the blanket. We had practised so many times, just to cement it in her mind, that it was no problem for her on the test day. Similarly, her emergency stop, when called from a wait, was spectacularly fast. In an unfamiliar place with other dogs present, her recall was really quick and she was up to full speed in a second and racing towards me. I shouted for her to go down, giving a clear hand signal, and she screeched to a halt and folded up into the down position. She is used to stopping on forgiving grass, and when I checked later, she had little pink scuff marks on her elbows where she had grated along the ground.

Next came the 'relaxed isolation' exercise. Knowing that she would chew through her lead if she noticed it, I carefully laid her down on top of it once I had attached it to the bench, as instructed, so she couldn't see it. Then I asked her to stay. I knew she could do a long down stay, but could she do it in a strange place with unfamiliar dogs around? I wasn't sure and that isn't a nice feeling when you are waiting out of sight, hoping she is being good but not able to see, especially given her previous history of panicking when left alone. I wondered if I had done enough practice.

I fretted and fussed behind the door in the hall where she couldn't see me and the minutes ticked slowly past. Then time was up and I peeped round the corner. She was still there, exactly as I had left her. I felt relief and a wave of emotion that she was so willing to have stayed put, safe in the knowledge that she wouldn't come to any harm and that I would return eventually. I went to her, stroking her neck gently and telling how clever she was. Her tail flickered on the ground and I fed her some sausage as soon as I heard the judge say that the exercise was over.

The rest of the test was uneventful. She waited patiently to eat the food in the bowl placed beside her until I gave the cue to eat, and her two-minute out-of-sight stay was easy. As I received our rosette and certificate, I wished I'd had a video of the downtrodden, difficult creature she used to be so that the judges could compare it with the bright, confident, responsive dog she was today. I was amazed and relieved we had brought her so far and proud that we hadn't given up during the terrible times when we thought there was no hope.

I thought about the long road of healing we had taken Chesil on as I drove her home. She had been such a smelly, aggressive, disruptive dog when we first got her that had distressed us and driven us to despair. Having no choice, we had struggled our way forward until she started to become better behaved and easier to live with. Gradually, she had become a dog that fitted easily into the family, one that we loved and which loved us and was no trouble to have around. I wondered what had made the most difference to her. We had certainly needed all my knowledge of behaviour control and animal learning in the early days to turn around her bad habits and make her into a dog we could live with. What had really made her turn the corner, however, was the love and acceptance she now felt being part of our lives and our family. It was this, above all else, that resulted in a dog that felt at ease with life and comfortable in its own skin.

We stopped at some traffic lights, and, having a little bit of time, I turned and pushed some of the remaining sausage through the bars of her cage. I felt she deserved it after how well she had done. She ate enthusiastically, but in her rush to get it all into her mouth at once, she accidently pushed a piece through the bars and out of reach. I put my hand down into the narrow gap between the cage and the car and pushed it back for her. She waited patiently until it was within reach and then took it and swallowed without chewing. I remembered a time when she didn't trust anyone enough to do that. She would have gone into a frenzy of aggression trying to keep my hand away from her food. Now she trusted me to deliver. She had learnt that humans are prepared to work with her and be cooperative. It was a really good example of how far she had come and encapsulated the difference between then and now.

When we got home, Grant was waiting to celebrate her achievements. He had cooked some chicken specially and Chesil and Spider enjoyed their unexpected treat. I put all the certificates and rosettes together on the kitchen table and they stayed there for days as a reminder of our amazing success with a dog that we had gradually transformed from a difficult dog that no one had wanted to a happy, well-behaved and much loved member of our family.

Epilogue

IT'S early in the morning and I'm standing in our bedroom looking out of the window. Spider is waiting patiently for me to finish doing what I need to do before I'm ready to present myself to the world and we can go for a walk. Grant is already up and is down at the end of our long drive checking on the trees he has recently planted. Chesil is with him. Her curiosity takes her towards the entrance that leads to the road to see what is outside. Seeing this, Grant moves towards her. I can see his hand signals clearly from where I stand as he asks her to come back to him. She trots back happily and walks beside him as he slowly walks back towards the house.

Holly appears on the drive, still in her nightclothes and looking for her father. She can see him but he's too close to the road for her to go down without getting dressed. Instead she calls Chesil, a long, high-pitched 'Cheeessie!' She is rewarded by Chesil racing up the drive as fast as she can go, legs flying, ears plastered back. She gets to

Holly at full speed and throws herself enthusiastically, but politely, into a sit. Holly fusses her for a while and then walks away. Excitement over, Chesil wanders off, sniffing the ground and then, finding a stick, lays down under a tree to chew it.

About the author

Other books written by Gwen Bailey and published by Hamlyn include: *The Perfect Puppy, Choosing the Right Dog For You, What is My Dog Thinking?, Puppy School: 7 Steps to the Perfect Puppy*, and *Why is My Dog Doing That?*

For more on Gwen Bailey's work and further information on dog behaviour issues, please visit www.gwenbailey.co.uk

Puppy School is a UK network of training classes for young puppies. Classes are of the highest standard and only kind, effective techniques are used. Puppies are 'educated' to have good manners, be friendly with other dogs and humans and respond to commands. For details of classes in your areas, visit: www.puppyschool.co.uk

For owner of dogs with behaviour problems who need further help and advice, please visit the Association of Pet Behaviour Counsellors website www.apbc.org.uk or contact your veterinary surgery for referral to a local practitioner.